**ACCOUNTING
FOR THE COST
OF PENSION PLANS**

ACCOUNTING
RESEARCH
STUDY NO. 8

# ACCOUNTING FOR THE COST OF PENSION PLANS

**By Ernest L. Hicks, CPA**
Partner
Arthur Young & Company

Published by the
American Institute of Certified Public Accountants, Inc.
666 Fifth Avenue     New York, New York   10019

*Copyright 1965 by the
American Institute of Certified Public Accountants, Inc.
666 Fifth Avenue, New York, N. Y. 10019*

*Publication of this study by the American Institute of Certified Public Accountants does not in any way constitute official endorsement or approval of the conclusions reached or the opinions expressed.*

# Table of Contents

|  | Page |
|---|---|
| DIRECTOR'S PREFACE | xiii |
| AUTHOR'S PREFACE | xv |

*Chapter*

1. SUMMARY AND CONCLUSIONS . . . . . . . . . . . . . . 1

    *Timing the Charges to Expense, 2*
     *Choice of Basis of Accounting, 2*
     *Applying the Accrual Basis, 3*
      *Actuarial cost methods, 3*
      *Normal cost, 4*
      *Past service cost, 4*
      *Increase in prior service cost upon amendment, 6*
      *Actuarial gains and losses, 7*
      *Unrealized appreciation (depreciation)
       of pension fund investments, 7*
      *Employee service before coverage, 8*
      *Interest on differences between pension
       cost accruals and contributions, 8*
      *Defined-contribution plans, 9*
     *Transition to Recommended Procedures, 10*
    *Presentation in Financial Statements, 11*
     *Amounts Appearing in the Balance Sheet, 12*
     *Disclosure, 12*
    *Other Considerations, 13*
     *Responsibility for Calculations of Pension Cost, 13*
     *Income Tax Allocation, 14*
     *Materiality, 14*
     *Comparability of Financial Statements, 14*
     *Pension Cost Incurred Outside the United States, 15*

| Chapter | Page |
|---|---|
| 2. THE PENSION ENVIRONMENT . . . . . . . . . . . . . | 16 |

    *Present Accounting Practices, 16*
        *Timing the Charges to Expense, 16*
        *Presentation in Financial Statements, 18*
    *Provisions of Pension Plans, 19*
        *Classifications of Plans, 19*
        *Documents, 20*
        *Eligibility, 21*
        *Retirement Age, 21*
        *Benefits, 22*
        *Credited Service, 23*
        *Vesting, 23*
        *Contributions by the Employer, 23*
        *Contributions by Employees, 24*
        *Limitation of Employer's Liability, 24*
    *Legal Status, 24*
    *Involvement in Actuarial Science, 25*
        *Actuarial Assumptions, 25*
        *Actuarial Cost Methods, 26*
        *Unrealized Appreciation (Depreciation) of Pension Fund Investments, 28*
    *Federal Income Tax Consequences, 28*
        *Deductibility of Contributions, 29*
        *Actuarial Cost Methods, 30*
        *Actuarial Assumptions, 30*

| 3. TIMING THE CHARGES TO EXPENSE . . . . . . . . . . . | 31 |

    *Underlying Concepts, 31*
    *Simplifying the Discussion, 32*
    *Choice of Basis of Accounting, 33*
        *Proposition A. The amount which should be recorded as the pension* expense *for a given accounting period is the amount* paid *for the period, 33*
        *Proposition B. There should not be an accounting requirement which would lead an employer to record expense under a pension plan in an amount exceeding the legal responsibility imposed by the plan, 37*
        *Conclusion on choice of basis of accounting, 38*
    *Applying the Accrual Basis, 39*
        *Actuarial Cost Methods, 40*

| Chapter | Page |
|---|---|

    Proposition C. *The* entry age normal method *is the only actuarial cost method acceptable for use in accounting for pension cost on the accrual basis,* 41
    Conclusion on actuarial cost methods, 43
  Normal Cost, 43
  Past Service Cost, 44
    Proposition D. *Past service cost should be charged to retained earnings at the inception of a pension plan,* 45
    Proposition E. *Past service cost should be charged to expense only to the extent funded (including amounts identified as "interest"),* 46
    Proposition F. *Past service cost should be charged in equal annual amounts (including "interest") over the average remaining service life, from the inception of the plan, of employees initially covered,* 49
    Proposition G. *Regardless of the actuarial method used in determining the normal cost, further accounting charges for the principal of past service cost should not be required* when the assets of the pension fund, at market value, and any pension liability on the employer's books are equal to or in excess of the value of "accrued benefits" *(a modification of Proposition F),* 50
    Conclusion on past service cost, 53
  Increase in Prior Service Cost upon Amendment, 55
    Proposition H. *When an amendment increases the benefits granted by a pension plan, the resulting increase in prior service cost should be charged directly to retained earnings as an adjustment of pension expense for prior years,* 56
    Conclusion on increase in prior service cost upon amendment, 56
  Actuarial Gains and Losses, 57
    Proposition I. *Actuarial gains and losses should be spread over the current year and future years,* 58
    Conclusion on actuarial gains and losses, 59

Unrealized Appreciation (Depreciation) of Pension Fund
   Investments, 61
   Proposition J. Appreciation of pension fund
      investments should not be recognized in
      calculations of pension cost unless realized
      through sale or other disposition
      of the investments, 62
   Proposition K. Appreciation of common stock investments in a pension fund should be recognized, but
      only to a limited extent, 64
   Conclusion on unrealized appreciation
      (depreciation) of pension fund
      investments, 65
Employee Service Before Coverage, 66
   Proposition L. Expense under a pension plan should
      not be accrued in respect of service by employees
      who may become eligible for coverage but who
      have not met eligibility requirements as to age,
      length of service, or both, 66
   Conclusion on employee service before
      coverage, 67
Interest on Differences Between Pension Cost Accruals
   and Contributions, 68
Types of Plans Not Previously Discussed, 71
   Certain Insured Plans, 71
   Defined-contribution Plans, 72
   Unfunded Plans, 73
Other Considerations, 73
   Responsibility for Calculations of Pension Cost, 73
   Income Tax Allocation, 74
   Materiality, 75
   Comparability of Financial Statements, 75
   Pension Cost Incurred Outside the United States, 76
Transition to Recommended Procedures, 77
   Principal Changes, 77
      Consistency in recording pension expense, 77
      Actuarial cost methods, 77
      Accruing past service cost, 77
      Increase in prior service cost upon amendment, 78
      Recognizing actuarial gains and losses, 78
      Appreciation (depreciation) of pension fund
         investments, 78
   Putting the Changes into Effect, 78
      Theoretical considerations, 79
      Practical considerations, 80
      Summation on transition, 82

Chapter                                                                     Page

4. PRESENTATION IN FINANCIAL STATEMENTS . . . . . . 83

    *Existing Guidelines,* 83
    *Disclosure in the Body of the Financial Statements,* 84
        *Balance Sheet,* 84
            *Unfunded prior service cost,* 84
            *Vested rights,* 85
        *Statement of Income,* 86
            *Charge for pension expense,* 86
            *Interest,* 86
    *Disclosure in a Note,* 87
    *Conclusions,* 89
        *Amounts Appearing in the Balance Sheet,* 89
        *Disclosure,* 89

COMMENTS OF B. RUSSELL THOMAS . . . . . . . . . . . . 90

COMMENTS OF W. A. WALKER . . . . . . . . . . . . . . . 91

*Appendix*

A. THE PENSION BACKGROUND. . . . . . . . . . . . . 93

    *Economic Basis of the Old-Age Problem,* 93
        *Population Trends,* 93
        *Employment Opportunities for the Aged,* 94
        *Capacity to Save for Old Age,* 94
        *Changed Concept of Filial Responsibility,* 95
    *Public Pension Program,* 95
        *Federal Old-Age, Survivors, and Disability Insurance,* 95
            *Coverage,* 95
            *Benefits,* 96
            *Financing,* 96
        *Federal Staff Retirement Plans,* 97
        *State and Local Retirement Systems,* 97
        *Other Public Pension Programs,* 98
    *The Private Pension Movement,* 98
        *Rationale,* 98
        *Forces Influencing the Growth of Private Pension Plans,* 100
            *Productivity of the employee group,* 100
            *Tax inducements,* 101
            *Pressure from organized labor,* 103
            *Social pressure,* 104

*Appendix* *Page*

B. PUBLIC POLICY AND PRIVATE PENSION PROGRAMS . . . . 105

   *Summary of Major Conclusions and Recommendations, 105*
     *Development of Private Retirement Plans, 105*
     *The Public Interest in Private Retirement Plans, 106*
     *Relation of Private Plans to the Public Retirement Program, 107*
     *Private Pensions, Labor Mobility, and Manpower Policy, 107*
     *Vesting, 108*
     *Funding for Financial Solvency, 109*
     *Portability and Insurance, 110*
     *Inequities Under the Tax Laws, 110*
     *Financial Aspects of Retirement Plans, 111*
     *Protecting the Interests of Employees in the Investments*
        *of Retirement Funds, 112*
     *Further Study and Research, 112*

C. ACTUARIAL TECHNIQUES . . . . . . . . . . . . . . 113

   *Funding Instruments and Funding Agencies, 113*
     *Contracts with Life Insurance Companies, 114*
     *Trust Agreements, 115*
   *Pension Plan Valuations, 115*
   *Actuarial Assumptions, 116*
     *Interest (Return on Funds Invested), 117*
     *Expenses of Administration, 117*
     *Benefits, 117*
       *Future compensation levels, 118*
       *Cost-of-living, 118*
       *Mortality, 118*
       *Retirement age, 119*
       *Withdrawal (turnover), 119*
       *Vesting, 120*
       *Social security benefits, 120*
     *Actuarial Gains and Losses, 120*
   *Funding Methods, 121*
     *Pay-As-You-Go, 122*
     *Terminal Funding, 123*
     *Unit Credit Method, 123*
            TABLE I, *124*
     *Entry Age Normal Method, 127*
       *Aggregate basis, 128*
       *Individual basis, 130*
       *Other considerations, 130*
     *Individual Level Premium Method, 131*

| Appendix | Page |
|---|---|

       *Aggregate Method, 132*
       *Attained Age Normal Method, 133*
    *Unrealized Appreciation (Depreciation) of Pension Fund*
       *Investments, 134*
    *Actuaries, 135*
       *Casualty Actuarial Society, 136*
       *Conference of Actuaries in Public Practice, 136*
       *Fraternal Actuarial Association, 136*
       *Society of Actuaries, 136*
       *Proposed New Association, 137*

D. GLOSSARY . . . . . . . . . . . . . . . . . 138

E. ACCOUNTING RESEARCH BULLETINS . . . . . . . . . . 149

SELECTED BIBLIOGRAPHY . . . . . . . . . . . . . . 157

# Director's Preface

The problems involved in accounting for the cost of pension plans are technical and complicated, and suggested solutions have been divergent. The AICPA committee on accounting procedure set forth its conclusions on some aspects of pension costs in Accounting Research Bulletins in 1948, 1953, and 1956 and had the item on its agenda when it was replaced by the Accounting Principles Board in 1959. The Board recognized that this area required further study and authorized a research project on pension costs.

A number of the problems in accounting for the cost of pension plans result from the different points of view and interests of many groups—employers, employees, accountants, actuaries, insurers, educators, government officials, analysts, and others. It is not always easy to distinguish the similarities and differences of expense accruals and funding, for example, or to isolate the effects of the somewhat conflicting interests of several of the groups. This study is concerned primarily, however, with the cost of pension plans in financial statements, and every attempt has been made to consider and analyze the effects of varying viewpoints.

The complexities of the problems and the variety of interests justify careful examination of this study and scrutiny of the reasons underlying the conclusions. The resulting evaluations will aid the Accounting Principles Board in its review of the study.

To expedite the work of the Accounting Research Division, several accounting firms have generously agreed that individual partners will be available to carry out accounting research studies. This is the first study to be completed on this basis. All who have an interest in the accounting problems of pension plans will benefit from the contribution of Ernest L. Hicks, the author, in preparing this study of an important topic, and the generosity of Arthur Young & Company, the firm of which he is a partner, in providing the necessary time.

Members of the project advisory committee have provided valuable assistance throughout the period of research and writing and have reviewed the manuscript. The committee approves publication of this accounting research study. Approval of publication does not necessarily imply concurrence with the contents and conclusions. The comments of B. Russell Thomas and W. A. Walker, members of the committee, on certain conclusions in the study are published following the last chapter (pages 90 to 92).

*New York, N. Y., May 1965*                                  REED K. STOREY
*Director of Accounting Research*

# Author's Preface

Accounting for the cost of pension plans has received a great deal of attention, particularly during the past twenty-five years. Dissatisfaction with present practices, expressed by accountants and others, led to this study. The study evaluates and compares the varying proposals that have been made and suggests solutions for the problems.

The research underlying this study has brought together the views of numerous accountants, actuaries, corporate executives and others, expressed in articles and books or obtained through interviews and correspondence. Some sixty major companies having pension plans provided information about the practical problems encountered in pension accounting, supplementing information obtained from other sources. Published financial statements were reviewed to determine present practices in accounting for pension cost and in disclosing related information.

The author is indebted to those who have stated their views in articles, in books, in correspondence or otherwise. A number of individuals have been particularly helpful. Paul Grady, formerly Director of Accounting Research of the American Institute of Certified Public Accountants, and Reed K. Storey, the present Director, have provided valuable counsel. So have the members of the project advisory committee. Present members are: Thomas G. Higgins, chairman, S. J. Huse, Alvin R. Jennings, Robert E. Johnson, Robert J. McDonald, John Peoples, B. Russell Thomas, W. A. Walker and Theodore O. Yntema. William M. Black, Arthur H. Dean, and Robert M. Trueblood also served on the advisory committee for part of the time the project was in process. Alexander Russ, formerly of the Institute staff, conducted interviews in the early stages of the project and accumulated information about accounting practices.

The author is particularly grateful to Frederick P. Sloat, whose guidance on actuarial matters throughout this study was indispensable. Mr. Sloat has been available for frequent consultations, has reviewed drafts of the study, and has made many helpful suggestions. In addition to Mr. Sloat and the actuaries serving on the project advisory committee, a number of other actuaries have provided encouragement and assistance.

Several individuals and organizations have kindly granted permission to include material in the study. Charles L. Trowbridge and the Society of Actuaries have permitted use of a table adapted from one appearing in an article written by Mr. Trowbridge and published in the *Transactions of the Society of Actuaries*. Professor Dan M. McGill, author of *Fundamentals of Private Pensions* (second edition); the publishers, Richard D. Irwin, Inc.; and the Pension Research Council have approved use of material taken from that book.

As the study neared completion, the President's Committee on Corporate Pension Funds and Other Private Retirement and Welfare Programs issued a report entitled *Public Policy and Private Pension Programs—A Report to the President on Private Employee Retirement Plans*. The report is not directly concerned with *accounting* for the cost of private pension plans. Nevertheless, many of its recommendations, if given effect, would have an important bearing on matters discussed in this study. A summary of the major conclusions and recommendations of the report is included in this study as an appendix.

A word about the organization of this study may be of value. Because the study is intended to be useful to readers having a variety of backgrounds and interests, some of the material appears in more than one section. Chapter 1 briefly summarizes the problems and states the conclusions reached. This material appears again in Chapters 3 and 4, accompanying an analysis of the accounting issues. All three chapters presuppose some familiarity with actuarial techniques. Actuarial techniques are reviewed briefly in Chapter 2 and are described in more detail in Appendix C. Those who are unfamiliar with such techniques may wish to read Appendix C before reading any of the numbered chapters.

This study could not have been brought to completion without the help of the persons named above and many others. Nevertheless, the responsibility for the conclusions reached and for the accuracy of the text is the author's alone.

*New York, N. Y., May 1965*                                     ERNEST L. HICKS

# 1

## Summary and Conclusions

United States companies have long been concerned with providing for the retirement of employees. This concern has increased markedly since the mid-1930's; commitments under private pension plans are now an important aspect of American business, and the funds accumulated to finance private pensions constitute significant economic factors.[1]

The practices of employers in accounting for the cost of pension plans have varied widely. A committee of the American Institute of Certified Public Accountants has issued two Bulletins dealing with the subject,[2] but many accountants and others have expressed dissatisfaction both with the Bulletins and with present practices. This study was undertaken to provide a basis for determining appropriate practice.

The expressions "pension" and "pension plan" have a variety of meanings. For the purposes of this study, therefore, a *pension plan* is defined as an arrangement whereby an employer provides benefits for retired employees which can be determined (or estimated) in advance

---

[1] Appendix A traces the development of pension plans in the United States.

[2] *Accounting Research Bulletin No. 43*, Chapter 13A, "Pension Plans—Annuity Costs Based on Past Service," 1953, and *Accounting Research Bulletin No. 47*, "Accounting for Costs of Pension Plans," 1956, reproduced in Appendix E.

from the provisions of a document or documents or from the employer's practices. The term thus comprehends, in addition to written plans, plans which may be inferred from the existence of a well defined, although unwritten, policy on the part of the employer regarding payment of retirement benefits. On the other hand, an employer's practice of making retirement payments in amounts determined arbitrarily at or after retirement to selected retired employees does not constitute a pension plan for purposes of this study. Profit-sharing plans, in which the employer's contributions are based on the employer's earnings, are also excluded; so are arrangements for deferred compensation of executives. Although all of these arrangements have some of the characteristics of pension plans, they constitute a separate field of study.

The central problem in accounting for the cost of pension plans concerns the *timing* of the employer's charges to expense. A second major issue concerns the *presentation* in the employer's financial statements of information concerning pension plans and pension cost. This chapter summarizes the issues and presents the conclusions reached in this study. The conclusions, developed in Chapters 3 and 4, flow from an analysis of diverse viewpoints presented in those chapters. Consequently, it is not practicable to restate the reasoning in this chapter. Page references are given, however, to sections in Chapters 3 and 4 wherein the issues are analyzed.

## TIMING THE CHARGES TO EXPENSE

### Choice of Basis of Accounting  (Ch. 3, p. 33)

With few exceptions, employers have, in the past, recognized the amount *paid* for a particular accounting period, either directly to pensioners for current benefits or to a funding agency for future benefits, as the pension *expense* for the period. (Ordinarily, the amount paid is also the amount deductible in the employer's Federal income tax return.) This accounting practice is commonly based on one of two premises: (1) that the nature of pension plans is such that an employer should record as pension expense only the amounts paid or (2) that the method used in arriving at the amount paid also arrives at an accounting charge appropriate for use in determining net income under fundamental accounting concepts. The first premise results in accounting on the *cash basis;* the second intends to conform to the *accrual basis.*

*It is a conclusion of this study that an employer's financial position and results of operations, to the extent affected by the cost of a pension plan, are fairly presented only if such cost is stated on the accrual basis.*

## Applying the Accrual Basis (Ch. 3, p. 39)

A recommendation for accrual accounting does not of itself provide sufficient guidance for determining the amount and timing of an employer's charges to expense for pension cost, since a number of significant questions arise in applying the accrual basis. The first is: What cost must be accounted for? Opposing views are embodied in the following antithetic descriptions of an acceptable minimum annual charge for expense under a pension plan:

> An appropriately assigned portion of the cost (present value) of *specific pension benefits* expected to become payable in the future to *specific persons.*

versus

> An amount such that, if similarly determined amounts were contributed annually to a fund, *the plan* would be enabled to remain in operation indefinitely.

The practical significance of the difference in viewpoints will become manifest as the discussion turns to (a) *actuarial cost methods,* which are used in calculating pension cost, and (b) *normal cost* and *past service cost,* of which pension cost is composed.

*Actuarial cost methods* (Ch. 3, p. 40)

Another important question in applying the accrual basis concerns the extent to which the several actuarial cost methods by which pension cost may be assigned to periods of time are acceptable for use in accrual accounting. The methods under consideration are those used at present in determining employers' payments which are charged to expense.[3]

*It is a conclusion of this study that the actuarial cost methods pres-*

---

[3] Actuarial cost methods are discussed in Appendix C (page 121). Because their primary use in the past has been in determining amounts to be paid, actuarial cost methods are referred to in Appendix C as "funding methods."

ently used in calculating payments under pension plans are acceptable for use in accrual accounting if they are applied in accordance with the other conclusions of the study. (*Pay-as-you-go* and *terminal funding* are unacceptable because they do not make provision for the cost of future retirement benefits during employees' periods of active service. They are not exceptions to the conclusion stated, however, because they are not considered to be actuarial cost methods.)

Because of the long-range nature of pension commitments and the extent of the uncertainties involved in estimating pension cost, this study prefers that pension expense be recorded as nearly as possible in level annual amounts, varied only to give effect to changes in facts. (Examples of the latter are variations in the level of employment, increases in pension benefits resulting from a plan amendment, and the effects of accounting for past service cost.) The actuarial cost method which most nearly accomplishes this objective is the entry age normal method, which is, therefore, preferred.

*Normal cost* (Ch. 3, p. 43)

*It is a conclusion of this study that provision should be made annually for the normal cost of a pension plan*—the cost assigned, under the actuarial cost method used, to years subsequent to the inception of the plan. Without significant exception, those who favor accrual accounting for pension cost will endorse this conclusion. This may be, however, the only aspect of pension cost accounting on which there is anything approaching unanimity, and it must be emphasized that even this consensus exists only among those who accept the accrual basis.

*Past service cost* (Ch. 3, p. 44)

If there is limited agreement on accounting for normal cost, there is extensive disagreement on accounting for past service cost—the cost assigned, under the actuarial cost method used, to years prior to the inception of a pension plan. A few would charge past service cost retroactively to the prior years. Others would charge such cost to expense in subsequent years, but only to the extent funded (including amounts identified as "interest"). Still others would bring such cost (and related charges for interest) into expense over a "reasonable period" following the inception of a pension plan. Those in this last group disagree as to the duration of the period in which an employer realizes the advantages associated with the past service element of a pension plan. Some in this group associate the employer's advantages with the remaining service lives of employees initially covered. Others believe the advantages are so nebulous that the employer should have wide latitude in selecting an accrual period. Proposals identifying the period range from a relatively short time—for example, ten years or the period of between eleven and twelve years which results from applying the Federal income tax rule limiting the annual deduction for past service cost to (generally) 10 per cent of the initial amount— to an indefinitely long time. If the period chosen is so long that it approaches infinity, the past service cost is not accrued at all, and only interest on the initial amount is charged. Among those who would limit accruals for past service cost to amounts equal to interest are those holding the view that the annual charge for pension expense should be the amount necessary to enable the plan to remain in operation (page 3). For many plans, an annual contribution comprising the normal cost and interest on the unfunded past service cost accomplishes this purpose.

*It is a conclusion of this study that past service cost should be taken into expense (together with related charges for interest) systematically over a reasonable period following the inception of a pension plan.*

The study has dealt separately with past service cost only because some of the actuarial techniques commonly used determine this element of pension cost separately. In concluding that past service cost should be taken into expense over a reasonable period following the inception of a pension plan, the study answers the question raised earlier in this chapter (page 3): What cost must be accounted for? The study accepts the view that the cost to be accounted for is the cost of *specific pension benefits* expected to become payable to *specific persons;* it does not accept the concept that the cost to be recognized is limited to an amount necessary to keep *the plan* in operation.

It has been proposed that accounting charges for past service cost under certain of the actuarial cost methods be terminated when the value of "accrued benefits" (determined under the unit credit method) has been fully accounted for. This proposal is unsatisfactory, for reasons given in the analysis of accounting arguments (Chapter 3, page 50). In declining to accept the proposal, however, the study does not necessarily require continued accrual of past service cost beyond the point stated. The study has concluded that the unit credit method is acceptable for accounting purposes. Consequently, a company using another method may change to the unit credit method, thus accomplishing the objective of limiting charges for past service cost. Disclosure in the event of a change in actuarial cost method is discussed in Chapter 4 (page 88).

The study has not brought to light criteria for identifying with certainty the period in which an employer realizes the diverse advantages of granting past service pensions. It seems clear, however, that in most instances the greater part of the advantage is related to the periods in which the employees who will receive pensions based on past service will complete their employment. Consequently, a weighted average of the remaining service lives of such employees should be a starting point in determining the accrual period. Because the period cannot be definitely identified, however, there should be flexibility. A reasonable range would seem to be from a minimum of ten years to a maximum of forty years. The minimum period of ten years is equal to the minimum for income tax purposes (if past service cost is paid in advance). Using a short period would make it easier for a company which expects to grant increased pension benefits, thus creating additional prior service cost, to approach the practical objective of maintaining level annual charges for pension cost. On the other hand, for many employers, using a long period would reduce the annual past service charge to a relatively inconsequential amount.

The study prefers that pension expense be recorded in level annual amounts. This objective is most nearly accomplished, as to past service cost, by taking such cost into expense in substantially equal annual amounts (including interest) over a reasonable period following the inception of a pension plan. Other systematic approaches, however, are acceptable. For example, some employers may prefer to accrue past service cost in diminishing annual amounts because the number of employees to whom such cost applies diminishes as employees retire.

*Increase in prior service cost upon amendment* (Ch. 3, p. 55)

When a pension plan is amended to increase retirement benefits, as often occurs, the change ordinarily applies to benefits measured by employment prior to the date of the amendment as well as to those measured by employment thereafter. The resulting increase in prior service cost is analogous to past service cost arising when a pension plan is adopted. The accounting question is whether such an increase in prior service cost should be treated as (a) an adjustment of pension expense for prior years or (b) a factor in determining pension expense for subsequent years.

*It is a conclusion of this study that an increase in prior service cost, resulting from an amendment of a pension plan increasing benefits, should be taken into expense (together with related charges for interest) systematically over a reasonable period following the effective date of the amendment.*

The foregoing conclusion necessarily parallels the conclusion for past service cost. Again, the appropriate accrual period cannot ordinarily be identified with certainty. Again, the average remaining service lives of the employees active at the date of the amendment should be a starting point.

In practice, an increase in prior service cost resulting from an amendment liberalizing benefits is sometimes treated in the actuarial calculations as additional normal cost for current and future years, sometimes as additional past service cost. The former treatment accomplishes the objective of accruing the additional cost over a reasonable period. The latter does so if the procedure followed for past service cost conforms with the conclusions of this study and if the remaining accrual period for past service cost is an appropriate period for taking the additional prior service cost into expense. If the remaining period is unduly short, it may be desirable to spread the combined amounts over a new period.

In rare instances, modification of a pension plan may result in a decrease in prior service cost, rather than an increase. The conclusion stated is applicable in such instances, but the effect would be reversed.

*Actuarial gains and losses* (Ch. 3, p. 57)

Actuarial gains and losses are an inevitable element of pension cost calculations, and the method of applying such adjustments may significantly affect the amount the employer records for pension expense. Two techniques for recognizing actuarial adjustments are in general use. The *immediate basis* (not ordinarily used at present for net losses) applies net gains to reduce pension expense for the year after the adjustment is determined. The *spread basis* applies a net gain or loss to current and future expense, either through the normal cost or through the past service cost.

*It is a conclusion of this study that actuarial gains and losses should in most instances be spread over the current year and future years.* Nevertheless, circumstances may arise in which spreading is not appropriate. In general, immediate recognition may be preferable for an adjustment resulting from a single occurrence not directly related to the operation of a pension plan and not in the ordinary course of the employer's business—for example, the closing of a plant, or a business combination.

*Unrealized appreciation (depreciation) of pension fund investments* (Ch. 3, p. 61)

Important questions in accounting for actuarial gains and losses are (1) whether unrealized appreciation of pension fund investments should be recognized and (2) if so, how. In many (perhaps most) pension plan valuations, unrealized appreciation is not recognized at present. For most pension funds, long-range depreciation of investment securities has not been a problem.

*It is a conclusion of this study that unrealized appreciation or depreciation of common stocks (and, in some instances, bonds and investments of other types) in a pension fund should be recognized systematically in estimating the employer's pension cost for accounting purposes.* The conclusion does not apply to amounts inuring to participants under a variable benefit pension plan.

In the case of investments other than common stocks, analysis will disclose whether it is more reasonable to believe that changes in value will ultimately be realized or to believe that they will not.

Several techniques are available for recognizing unrealized appreciation or depreciation of investments of a pension fund. This study favors the use of a procedure which does not give undue weight to short-term market fluctuations.[4]

*Employee service before coverage* (Ch. 3, p. 66)

Under some pension plans, employees are eligible for coverage when they are hired if they are within the classification of employees entitled to participate (for example, members of a certain bargaining unit); under other plans, there are additional requirements as to age or length of service or both. Some plans, on the other hand, state the conditions an employee must meet in order to be eligible to receive retirement benefits but otherwise do not deal with coverage.

*It is a conclusion of this study that present employees who may reasonably be expected to become participants in a pension plan should be included in calculations of the cost of the plan for accounting purposes.*

In practice, it may be desirable to exclude employees during an initial period of service in which turnover is high (for example, three years). This may simplify the calculations without significantly changing the annual amount.

*Interest on differences between pension cost accruals and contributions* (Ch. 3, p. 68)

The actuarial cost methods used in assigning the cost of a pension plan to periods of time, whether for accounting or for funding pur-

---

[4] For a discussion of procedures, see Appendix C (page 134).

poses, assume that contributions by the employer (and in some instances by employees) will provide part of the money needed to pay benefits and that earnings on pension fund investments (called *interest* for simplicity) will provide the balance. If the employer's contributions exceed those assumed, the portion of the total cost which will be met by interest increases, and the employer's future contributions are correspondingly reduced. If, on the other hand, the employer's contributions are less than those assumed, the interest which would otherwise have been earned on fund investments must eventually be contributed by the employer if the expectations of the procedure adopted for accounting purposes are to be fulfilled.

*It is a conclusion of this study that, if the contributions to a pension fund differ from the accounting charges, the latter should include (or be reduced by) interest on the difference between the actual pension fund and a theoretical fund which would have been produced on the basis of the accounting charges.*

*Defined-contribution plans* (Ch. 3, p. 72)

Defined-contribution plans require special consideration. Under one type, known as a *money-purchase plan,* the employer's contributions are determined for, and allocated with respect to, specific individuals, usually as a percentage of compensation. The benefits for each employee are the amounts which can be provided by the sums contributed for him. Under this type of plan, the employer's contributions *for* a given period (not necessarily those made *in* the period) are the proper amounts to be charged to expense.

The other, more common, type bears the name *defined-contribution plan.* It states the pension benefits or the method of determining them, as does a defined-benefit plan. A *defined-contribution plan,* however, is ordinarily drawn up to accompany a separate agreement that provides a formula for calculating the employer's contributions (for example, a fixed amount for each ton produced or for each hour worked, or a fixed percentage of compensation). Initially, the benefits stated in the plan are those which the contributions expected to be made by the employer can provide. In relating benefits and contributions, one of the actuarial cost methods described in Chapter 2 (page 26) is used. The calculation may be made (1) on the basis that the defined contributions are to include amortization of past service cost over a selected period (such as 30 years) or (2) on the basis that the defined contributions are to include only interest on the past service cost. Ordinarily, if the defined contributions include an allowance for amortization of past service cost, it would be unlikely for indications to exist at the inception of a *defined-contribution plan* necessitating an accrual pattern differing from the payment pattern.

If the defined contributions subsequently appear to be inadequate or excessive for the purpose of *funding* the stated benefits on the basis originally contemplated (for example, because of a change in the level of the employer's operations), either the contributions or the benefits (or both) may be adjusted in subsequent negotiations. Under such circumstances, or if the defined contributions differ from an accounting charge conforming with the criteria set out in this study, determining an appropriate accounting accrual will require careful analysis based on the facts of each situation.

## Transition to Recommended Procedures   (Ch. 3, p. 77)

Some employers at present account for the cost of pension plans in conformity with the conclusions of this study. Others will change their procedures in varying degrees if they adopt the study's conclusions. In discussing the problem of how to put into effect any necessary changes in procedures, the following solutions should be considered:

**1.** As of the date of change, determine the cumulative difference between the provisions for pension expense previously made under procedures not meeting the criteria developed in this study and provisions which would have been made in conformity with the study's criteria. The amount may be either a charge (if prior provisions have been inadequate) or a credit (if prior provisions have been excessive). Account for this amount (giving appropriate consideration to the effect of income tax) as an adjustment of results of operations for prior years (for purposes of this discussion, it will be assumed that such an adjustment would be carried directly to retained earnings)[5] or as an adjustment of other prior transactions. As an illustration of an adjustment of the latter type, if employees have become participants in the plan as a result of a merger or other business combination, it may be appropriate to apply part of the "cumulative difference" as a correction of the entries made to record the business combination (see the discussion on page 60). In years following the date of change, charge

---

[5] Adjustments of prior years' operating results are discussed in *Accounting Research Bulletin No. 43*, Chapter 8, "Income and Earned Surplus," 1953.

operations with pension expense determined in conformity with the criteria developed in this study.

**2.** As of the date of change, determine the "cumulative difference" described in Solution 1. In subsequent years, charge operations with an amount consisting of (a) pension expense determined in conformity with the criteria developed in this study and (b) an allocated portion of such "cumulative difference." Because the latter factor would in effect be a correction of results of operations for years prior to the date of change, the criteria developed in this study would have no significance in selecting the number of future years to which this element would be allocated.

**3.** As of the date of change, determine the amount of prior service cost not previously funded or otherwise accounted for (in most instances, this amount will be the unfunded prior service cost). In subsequent years, charge operations with an amount consisting of (a) normal cost determined in conformity with criteria developed in this study and (b) an allocated portion of prior service cost not previously accounted for. The latter factor would be determined substantially as if the plan had been adopted or amended as of the date of change. It would include (as an unidentified increase or reduction) a portion of the "cumulative difference" described in Solution 1.

None of the solutions is satisfactory on both theoretical and practical grounds. Further, resolution of the issue must be predicated upon resolution of a broader question—the general question of retroactive application of changes in accounting principles—which is beyond the purview of an inquiry into methods of accounting for the cost of pension plans. Consequently, this study does not propose a conclusion as to the procedure which should be adopted in putting into effect the criteria developed in the study for assigning pension cost to periods of time. However, except that precedent for *requiring* retroactive adjustments is lacking and except in special circumstances such as those of companies in regulated industries and companies having cost reimbursement contracts, the study views retroactive adjustment (Solution 1) as preferable.

## PRESENTATION IN FINANCIAL STATEMENTS

Questions of presentation may be discussed in relation to (1) information which should appear in the body of the financial statements and (2) information which should appear in notes. Some information, of course, may appropriately be presented in either category.

### Amounts Appearing in the Balance Sheet  (Ch. 4, p. 84)

It is sometimes suggested that the amount of unfunded prior service cost (in particular, the amount of unfunded past service cost) of a pension plan represents a liability which should be shown in the employer's balance sheet. Those who would so present past service cost at the inception of a plan might also present a deferred charge of equal amount, the latter to be amortized by charges to expense in succeeding years. It is sometimes suggested, also, that the present value of pension rights which have vested in employees, unless previously funded, should appear as a liability.

*It is a conclusion of this study that the unfunded prior service cost of a pension plan is not a liability which must be shown in the balance sheet of an employer. Ordinarily, the amount to be shown for pension cost in the employer's balance sheet is the difference between the amount which has been charged to expense in accordance with the recommendations of this study and the amount which has been paid. If, as may occur in rare instances, participants' vested rights are a liability of the employer, the unfunded present value should appear as a liability; if the employer accounts for the cost of the plan in conformity with the recommendations of this study, the amount should be carried forward as a deferred charge to operations.*

### Disclosure  (Ch. 4, p. 87)

Opinions vary widely as to the nature and extent of information concerning pension plans which may be useful to readers of financial statements. At present, the amount of pension cost in expense, the amount of unfunded prior service cost, the basis for funding such cost, and a brief explanation when a pension plan is adopted or amended may appear in notes. Some suggest that more information should be disclosed.

*It is a conclusion of this study that routine pension disclosures should not ordinarily be necessary in the financial statements of companies whose accounting for pension cost conforms with the recommendations of the study. If, however, a change in an accounting practice or an accounting change necessitated by altered conditions affects the com-*

*parability of the employer's financial statements as between accounting periods, the change and its effect should be disclosed.*

## OTHER CONSIDERATIONS

### Responsibility for Calculations of Pension Cost   (Ch. 3, p. 73)

The calculations required in assigning the cost of a pension plan to periods of time involve complicated actuarial considerations. Consequently, actuaries play a leading role. Nevertheless, the corporate executive responsible for the employer's financial statements ordinarily bears the responsibility for the amount of pension cost recorded. In exercising this responsibility, the executive may discuss with the actuary the choice of actuarial cost method and actuarial assumptions. After the calculations have been made, the executive may review them. In both instances, his objective would be to satisfy himself that the actuarial cost method used is acceptable for accounting purposes, that the actuarial assumptions, *taken together*, are reasonable, and that both the actuarial cost method and the assumptions have been applied in a manner acceptable for accounting purposes.[6]

---

[6] The responsibility of independent public accountants for pension cost in financial statements they examine is an *auditing* matter and, hence, is not considered in detail in this study on *accounting* for the cost of pension plans. Some commentators have implied that it is inappropriate for independent public accountants to inquire into the factors underlying an actuary's recommendation as to the amount to be charged to expense for pension cost. These commentators may not be fully aware that independent public accountants, in discharging their overall responsibility for reporting on financial statements, must frequently evaluate conclusions of experts on whose judgment a client's management has relied. It is usual, for example, to discuss with engineers their estimates of the cost of completing complicated contracts, to inquire of lawyers as to the possible outcome of important legal matters and to ascertain the basis on which tax counsel (if employed) has estimated tax liability. An independent public accountant has the same degree of responsibility for pension cost that he has for other financial statement elements of comparable materiality and may appropriately discuss the pension calculations with the actuary. In general, his objective would be the same as that of the financial executive responsible for the financial statements. In pursuit of this objective, he might examine the actuary's calculations to the extent necessary to confirm his understanding of the procedure followed.

### Income Tax Allocation (Ch. 3, p. 74)

In the past, the amounts which employers have deducted for pension expense in their Federal income tax returns have in most instances equalled the accounting charges because both have been based on the amounts paid. If the conclusions of this study are adopted, tax return deductions for pension expense may more frequently differ from accounting charges because the former presumably will continue to equal payments, while the latter may not.

When such differences occur, taxable income for the current year is greater or less than if the accounting method followed in the financial statements had been followed in the tax return as well. Ordinarily there is a reasonable expectation that taxable income for subsequent years will be correspondingly less or greater. Under present practice, such circumstances usually result in income tax allocation.

### Materiality (Ch. 3, p. 75)

The relative significance of the matters considered in this study may be expected to vary from employer to employer and from year to year for a particular employer. The study intends, however, to deal only with situations wherein the matters at issue are important. Materiality, while not specifically mentioned, is an implicit factor in each phase of the study; none of the conclusions reached is intended to apply when the amounts involved are so small that in fact it does not matter how they are handled.

### Comparability of Financial Statements (Ch. 3, p. 75)

A general objective of the research program of which this study is part is to narrow areas of difference and inconsistency in accounting practice. In the minds of many, this objective means enhancing the degree to which the financial statements of different companies are comparable by eliminating accounting differences (whether in principles, practices or methods) not justified by differences in circumstances. If comparability, in this sense, were to be acknowledged as an objective, the conclusions of the study (for example, the conclusion that any of several actuarial cost methods may appropriately be used in determining pension expense) would require reappraisal.

## Pension Cost Incurred Outside the United States  (Ch. 3, p. 76)

For the most part, this study has analyzed issues in terms of pension practices in the United States. Many U. S. companies, however, incur pension expense in other countries, either through divisions or through subsidiaries. Although there are variations, practices in other countries concerning private pension plans are generally comparable with U. S. practices. The conclusions reached in this study are intended to apply to pension cost incurred in other countries as well as in the United States.

# 2

# The Pension Environment

The environment in which accounting principles—or rules, or guidelines, or practices, or procedures—are developed is complex and diverse. For pension cost, the environment includes the present accounting practices of business, the forms of agreements used, legal considerations, actuarial techniques, the pertinent provisions of the Federal income tax laws and regulations, and other factors such as the influence exerted by labor unions. Certain aspects of the pension environment will be discussed in this chapter.

### PRESENT ACCOUNTING PRACTICES

### Timing the Charges to Expense

An employer's *payments* under a pension plan may be determined in a variety of ways. The practices fall, however, into two general classes. Some employers make periodic pension payments directly to retired employees; this procedure is called *pay-as-you-go*. Other employers make advance payments for future pension benefits to a *funding agency* (for example, a trustee or an insurance company). The methods of determining payments to a funding agency may vary widely from employer to employer and, for some employers, from year to year. Typically, however, an amount is paid for (a) current service cost (normal cost) and (b) past service cost. In some instances this latter segment is intended to cover only interest on the past service cost, while in others the intent is to amortize past service cost over a period of time, which may typically range from twelve to thirty years.

With few exceptions, employers have, in the past, recognized the amount *paid* for a particular accounting period, either directly to pensioners for current benefits or to a funding agency for future benefits, as the pension *expense* for the period. (Ordinarily, the amount paid is also the amount deductible in the employer's Federal income tax return.) This accounting practice is commonly based on one of two premises: (1) that the nature of pension plans is such that an employer should record as pension expense only the amounts paid or (2) that the method used in arriving at the amount paid also arrives at an appropriate accounting charge for determining net income. The first results in accounting on the *cash basis;* the second intends to conform to the *accrual basis.*

When an employer accounts for pension cost on the cash basis, the charge to operations (that is, the amount paid) may be influenced by factors not properly considered in a theoretically sound determination of financial position and results of operations, such as the availability of cash or the level of the employer's earnings before deducting pension cost. In some years, an employer using the cash basis may show a relatively small pension expense because the amount of the payment is reduced or may show no pension expense because there is no payment.

Many companies which recognize pension cost on the cash basis are, by coincidence or intent, also following the accrual basis. But accounting principles generally accepted at the present time do not require use of the accrual basis for pension cost. Therefore, even those companies which coincidentally use the accrual basis may revert to cash basis accounting if conditions arise which make accrual accounting inconvenient.

The practices described have arisen under the influence of *Accounting Research Bulletin No. 47*, "Accounting for Costs of Pension Plans," issued in 1956 by the committee on accounting procedure of the American Institute of Certified Public Accountants.[1] In *ARB 47,* the committee expressed a preference for a method under which

---

[1] *ARB 47* is reproduced in Appendix E. The committee on accounting procedure was replaced in 1959 by the Institute's Accounting Principles Board, but most of the Bulletins issued by the committee, including *ARB 47,* remain in effect.

employers would (1) systematically accrue pension cost based on current and future services during the expected period of active service of the covered employees and (2) charge off cost based on past services over some reasonable period on a systematic and rational basis not causing distortion of the operating results in any one year. Widely varying viewpoints as to the length of the period to be used were reported in the Bulletin, but no opinion was expressed as to what constituted a reasonable period.

Although the committee indicated a preference for the method described above, it recognized an alternative method "for the present" and "as a minimum." Under the alternative method, financial statements should "reflect accruals which equal the present worth... of pension commitments... to the extent that pension rights have vested in the employees, reduced, in the case of the balance sheet, by any accumulated trusteed funds or annuity contracts purchased."

A number of companies have been influenced by the approval given to this "minimum" procedure. Some have charged to expense annually only the increase in the present value of vested pension rights. Others, whose payments in most years have conformed with the "preferred" method set forth in *ARB 47*, have used the "minimum" procedure in one or more years—that is, payments for pensions (and recorded expense) have been eliminated or reduced because the amount in the pension fund exceeded the present worth of vested benefits.

*ARB 47* also provided that the cost of pension benefits based on service prior to the adoption of a pension plan should not be charged to retained earnings at the inception of the plan.[2] This provision has been followed almost universally.

## Presentation in Financial Statements

Variations in the nature and extent of the information appearing in financial statements about pension plans and pension cost are less marked than the variations in determining charges to expense. Financial statements in reports to stockholders may include some or all of the following information, ordinarily in a note: (1) the amount of pension expense for the period (in some cases showing separately the amount for past service cost), (2) the basis for funding past service

---

[2] This position was originally expressed in *Accounting Research Bulletin No. 36*, "Pension Plans—Accounting for Annuity Costs Based on Past Services," 1948. *ARB 36* was incorporated in *ARB 43* as Chapter 13A, 1953. These statements dealt only with past service cost.

cost and (3) the amount of unfunded past service cost at the close of the period. In the year in which a pension plan is adopted, or amended to a material extent, a brief explanation may appear.

Financial statements which include the information just described conform with the disclosure requirements of *ARB 47*. Because of the requirements of the Securities and Exchange Commission's Regulation S-X,[3] disclosure in financial statements filed with the Commission is ordinarily somewhat more extensive than disclosure in annual reports to stockholders.

## PROVISIONS OF PENSION PLANS

The terms of a pension plan reflect the interaction of many factors. Some of these relate to the employees—for example, whether they are represented by a labor union, their average age and length of service, and their willingness and ability to set aside funds for their own retirement. Other factors relate to the employer—for example, the company's ability to finance pension benefits and the management's point of view as to how large benefits should be. As a result, provisions vary widely. The following discussion concerns those variations most likely to have accounting significance.

### Classifications of Plans

For purposes of discussion it is convenient to classify pension plans according to certain characteristics—primarily those flowing from specific plan provisions. A *negotiated plan* is one which results from collective bargaining, while a *unilateral plan* is one established by an employer without negotiation. A *multi-employer plan* (ordinarily a negotiated plan) is one established for the benefit of employees of two or more employers. A *pattern plan* is a form of plan negotiated with various employers by an international union, usually with relatively minor variations. Under an *unfunded plan,* payments are made di-

---

[3] Rule 3-19, entitled "General Notes to Balance Sheets," imposes the following requirement for disclosure: "(e) Pension and retirement plans—(1) A brief description of the essential provisions of any employee pension or retirement plan shall be given. (2) The estimated annual cost of the plan shall be stated. (3) If a plan has not been funded or otherwise provided for, the estimated amount that would be necessary to fund or otherwise provide for the past service cost of the plan shall be disclosed."

rectly to retired employees as they become due; under a *funded plan*, the employer sets aside funds for future pension benefits by making payments to a *funding agency*. If the funding agency is an insurance company, the plan is an *insured plan;* if a trustee, a *trust fund plan.* A *defined-benefit plan* states either the benefits to be received by employees after retirement or the method of determining the benefits; the employer's contributions are based on actuarial estimates of the amounts necessary to provide the benefits expected to become payable. The more common type of *defined-contribution plan* also states the benefits or the method of determining them; this type of plan, however, is ordinarily drawn up to accompany a separate agreement which provides a formula for calculating the employer's contributions (for example, a fixed amount for each ton produced or for each hour worked, or a fixed percentage of compensation). Initially, the benefits stated in the plan are those which the contributions expected to be made by the employer can provide. If later the contributions are found to be inadequate or excessive for the purpose of funding the stated benefits on the basis originally contemplated (for example, because of a change in the level of operations), either the contributions or the benefits (or both) may be adjusted in subsequent negotiations. A *money-purchase plan* is a type of defined-contribution plan in which the employer's contributions are determined for, and allocated with respect to, specific individuals, usually as a percentage of compensation. The benefits for each employee are the amounts which can be provided by the sums contributed for him. Under a *contributory plan*, employees bear part of the cost (in some plans on a voluntary basis with increased benefits); under a *noncontributory plan*, the employer pays the entire cost.

## Documents

A pension plan may be expressed through one or more of several different kinds of documents. In some cases, for example, the plan is contained in a contract with an insurance company, and the contract also provides the means of purchasing pension benefits (for example, annuities). In other cases, the *funding instrument* (such as a group annuity contract or a trust agreement) may be separate from the document containing the plan. In a trust fund plan, the trustee may in turn purchase insurance or annuity policies. A negotiated plan may involve several documents. For example, a general labor contract covering such matters as wages and working conditions may incorporate a pension plan by reference. The plan itself may be expressed in a separate document, and there may also be a trust agreement and, perhaps, an insurance contract or contracts.

## Eligibility

Some pension plans cover all of a company's employees. In most plans, however, an employee must meet certain requirements in order to be eligible for coverage. Thus, a plan may cover only those employees who are members of a particular bargaining unit, those who receive a salary or those who receive an hourly wage. Under some plans (ordinarily negotiated ones) an employee in a given classification may be eligible for coverage immediately upon hiring. Under other plans he may become eligible when he reaches a specified age (typically in the range of twenty-five to thirty-five years) and has accumulated a specified number of years of *service* (years of employment—typically in the range of two to five years). Some plans, on the other hand, state the conditions an employee must meet in order to be eligible to receive retirement benefits but otherwise do not deal with coverage. Many plans have a maximum age limitation. For example, an employee who has attained age fifty-five by the time he is hired or, perhaps, by the time he has accumulated the number of years of service otherwise necessary to qualify, may be ineligible for coverage.

## Retirement Age

Most plans provide an age (sixty-five is typical) at which employees normally will retire. Under some plans, employees may continue to work after the normal retirement age, ordinarily subject to the employer's approval.

Under most plans, employees who have accumulated a specified number of years of service and have attained a specified age may choose to retire in advance of the normal retirement age. Under these circumstances, the pension is usually less than it would have been had the employee continued to work until the normal retirement age.

Under most plans, an employee unable to work by reason of physical or mental disability may retire under the early retirement provision. In some plans, disability retirement benefits are available at an earlier age or with fewer years of service and may exceed the early retirement benefit.

## Benefits

The benefits to which employees or their beneficiaries may become entitled under pension plans vary widely. The basic benefit, of course, is the pension, usually beginning at the employee's retirement date and payable monthly thereafter for the remainder of his life. Some plans also provide death benefits. A death benefit after retirement may take the form of a provision that pension payments will continue for a specified period even though the employee does not survive the period.

Formulas used in determining monthly payments are diverse. In some plans, the payment is the same for all retired employees (for example, $100 per month). In plans for hourly employees, the benefit is typically a specified amount per month (for example, $4) for each year of credited service. In plans for salaried employees, on the other hand, the benefit is more often related to compensation. For example, an employee may receive each year a pension credit equal to a specified percentage (such as 2 per cent) of his earnings for the year. In such a case, the pension is, in effect, equal to the specified percentage of the employee's average earnings for the entire period considered. In other unilateral plans, the pension for each year of service is a percentage (such as 1.5 per cent) of the employee's average annual earnings during a specified period. The period may, for example, be the final ten years of employment or the five consecutive years of highest compensation in the final ten years of employment.

In some pension plans, the retirement benefits otherwise specified may be increased from time to time to provide a measure of protection of the purchasing power of the benefits. In a *cost-of-living plan*, the benefits are adjusted to reflect variations in a specific index, such as the Consumer Price Index of the United States Bureau of Labor Statistics. In an *equity annuity plan*, the periodic benefit (or, more often, one-half of the benefit) is dependent on the investment experience of a specific portfolio containing equity securities.

In some instances social security benefits reduce the benefits payable under the employer's pension plan. In some plans the tie-in with social security is accomplished by applying different percentages to earnings above and below the social security earnings maximum (in 1964, $4,800 per year).

Some plans provide minimum and maximum payments. Maximums may be stated in absolute terms or as a limitation on the number of years of credited service considered in determining benefits. In some plans there are separate formulas for benefits based on past service and for those based on service after the plan is adopted.

## Credited Service

The number of years of service credited to an employee may be significant in determining both his entitlement to benefits and their amount. Ordinarily, credited service begins to accumulate when the employee becomes eligible for coverage. In some cases, however, some or all of the years of service required for eligibility for coverage are also years of service for determining both eligibility to retire and the amount of the pension. For example, in a plan under which employees become eligible for coverage when they reach age thirty and have accumulated five years of service, an employee hired at age twenty-eight would accumulate three of his years of qualifying service after attaining age thirty. In some plans these three years would be counted as credited service; in others they would not.

## Vesting

An employee's right to receive a present or future pension benefit *vests* when his right eventually to receive the benefit is *no longer* contingent on his remaining in the service of the employer. (Other conditions, such as inadequacy of the pension fund, may prevent the employee from receiving the vested benefit.)

Almost without exception, the right to receive pension benefits for life vests in employees when they retire. In addition, under many plans an employee's right to a pension, ordinarily beginning at normal retirement age, vests when he has accumulated a specified number of years of service or has reached a stated age, or both. Under graded vesting, the *initial* vested right may be to receive in the future a stated percentage of a pension based on the number of years of accumulated credited service; *thereafter,* the percentage may increase with the number of years of service or of age until the right to receive the entire benefit has vested. Early retirement, discussed previously, is a form of vesting.

## Contributions by the Employer

Some plans specify the manner in which benefits are to be financed. For example, the employer may agree to purchase annuities or to make actuarially determined contributions to a trust. Some negotiated plans specify an amortization period for past service cost.

## Contributions by Employees

Under *contributory plans*, employees bear part of the cost. In some contributory plans, employees wishing to be covered must contribute; in others, employee contributions are voluntary and result in increased benefits.

Employees who withdraw from coverage under a contributory plan before retirement are entitled to receive the amount they have contributed, usually with interest, and in most instances at the time of withdrawal. The amount may, however, be payable at a later date either as a lump sum or in the form of an annuity, the latter ordinarily beginning at the normal retirement date.

## Limitation of Employer's Liability

Almost all pension plans contain one or more provisions intended to limit the legal liability of the employer. Most plans provide that the obligation of the employer is limited to amounts previously contributed to a trust or to an insurance company and give the employer the right to terminate the plan at any time. A negotiated plan, however, is usually kept in force for a specific period (terms of from two to five years are typical) by a separate agreement between employer and employees. Under a negotiated plan, the employer typically agrees to provide benefits, determined according to a stated formula, to employees who retire during the term of the agreement or who have retired under previous agreements. The employer may also agree to fund currently the benefits to become payable in the future to employees who retire during the term of the agreement.

## LEGAL STATUS

Pension plan provisions intended to limit the liability of the employer were described in the preceding section. Some writers[4] suggest that, whether or not there are provisions such as those described, the issue

---

[4] See Benjamin Aaron, *Legal Status of Employee Benefit Rights Under Private Pension Plans,* 1961, and Edwin W. Patterson, *Legal Protection of Private Pension Expectations,* 1960.

of the enforceability of employees' claims under pension plans is not settled. They point out that the number of relevant cases decided by courts is comparatively small and that the cases reported do not appear to interpret pension plan provisions uniformly. Among the questions remaining to be resolved are: Does a unilateral plan create a contract? If so, who are the contracting parties? Are pensions, in effect, deferred wages? What are the employee's rights if the pension fund is inadequate to provide the benefits stated in the plan?

## INVOLVEMENT IN ACTUARIAL SCIENCE[5]

The cost of a pension plan to be recognized currently by an employer is ordinarily expressed in terms of the present value of retirement benefits expected to be paid in the future. The calculations require the skills of an actuary.

### Actuarial Assumptions

Actuarial determinations of pension cost are necessarily estimates, since in making them actuaries must assign values to a number of significant uncertainties concerning future events. In doing so, they use factors called *actuarial assumptions.* Although these factors do not affect the actual (ultimate) cost of the plan, they have an important effect on present estimates of the cost. Some of the important actuarial assumptions are: (1) the rate of return to be earned on pension fund investments, (2) employees' future compensation, (3) mortality of employees, both before and after retirement, (4) rates of disability, (5) the age at which employees will retire and (6) the proportion of present employees who will withdraw from the plan before retirement. Whether a particular assumption applies depends primarily on the terms of the particular plan.

Actual events seldom coincide with actuarial assumptions. As a result, the assumptions may be changed from time to time as experience or judgment dictates. Further, whether or not the assumptions as to events in the future are changed, it may be necessary to recognize periodically the effect of differences between actual prior experience and the assumptions used in the past. In either event, the resulting

---

[5] For a more detailed discussion of actuarial techniques, see Appendix C (page 113).

adjustments, called *actuarial gains* and *actuarial losses,* are recognized immediately in some calculations but are spread over the current year and future years in others.

## Actuarial Cost Methods[6]

Any of several different *actuarial cost methods* (also called *funding methods*) may be used in determining an employer's payments under a pension plan.[7] The actuarial cost methods have in common the objective of making provision for future retirement benefits during employees' periods of active service. (*Pay-as-you-go* and *terminal funding* are not considered to be actuarial cost methods. In the former, the employer makes benefit payments directly to retired employees. In the latter, the employer makes payments only when employees retire; the amount, as to each employee, is usually the present value of his pension.) Although similar in objective, the methods differ significantly in approach and may produce widely varying results.

Pension cost is sometimes classified between *normal cost* and *past*

---

[6] The Committee on Pension and Profit-Sharing Terminology of The American Risk and Insurance Association has proposed new classifications and terminology for actuarial cost methods (funding methods). The proposed new terminology is compared below with the related terms most commonly employed in present practice and used in this study:

| *Proposed new terminology* | *Terms used in this study* |
|---|---|
| Accrued benefit cost method | Unit credit method |
| Projected benefit cost methods: | |
|   Individual level cost methods: | |
|     Without supplemental liability | Individual level premium method |
|     With supplemental liability | Entry age normal method (individual basis) |
|   Aggregate level cost methods: | |
|     Without supplemental liability | Aggregate method |
|     With supplemental liability | Attained age normal method; entry age normal method (aggregate basis) |
| Supplemental liability | Past service cost; prior service cost |

It should be noted that the word "level," as used in the new terminology, refers to the cost recognized for each participant in successive periods, rather than to the employer's total cost for the periods.

[7] The extent to which the various actuarial cost methods may appropriately be used in assigning pension cost to periods of time for accounting purposes is discussed in Chapter 3 (page 40).

*service cost.*[8] The former is the cost which the actuarial method chosen assigns to years after the inception of the pension plan; the latter is the cost which the method chosen assigns to years before the plan came into existence. When past service cost is determined separately, the employer's annual payment ordinarily includes the normal cost and an amount for past service cost. The latter may represent only interest on the unfunded past service cost, or it may also include an amount to reduce the unfunded balance. A past service payment of the latter type may, for example, be the sum necessary to amortize the past service cost in level annual amounts (including interest) over a stated period, such as twenty-five years.

Under the *unit credit method*,[9] pension cost is assigned to periods of time in direct relation to units of service. As an example, if a plan provides benefits of $4 per month for each year of credited service, the normal cost for a particular employee for a particular year is the present value (usually adjusted for withdrawal and for mortality before retirement) of an annuity of $4 per month beginning at the employee's anticipated retirement date and continuing throughout his life. The past service cost under this method for a particular employee is the present value at the inception of the plan of a similar annuity equal to $4 multiplied by the number of years of credited service prior to the inception date. For most plans, the annual *normal cost* determined by this method tends to increase, at least in the early years. (The increase may, however, be camouflaged by the effects of other factors.)

Thus, the unit credit method assigns only the cost of benefits which have *accrued* (in the limited sense that the units of employee service on which the benefits are based have been rendered). In contrast, the other actuarial cost methods look forward. That is, they apportion to past, present and future periods the entire cost of an employee's *projected* benefits without regard to the periods during which the service on which the benefits are based has been or will be rendered.

In the *entry age normal method*,[10] the assumption is made that every employee entered the plan at the time of employment or at the earliest time he would have been eligible if the plan had been in existence. The normal cost is the annual contribution necessary to spread the pension cost for present employees in level annual amounts over the period from the theoretical entry dates to the dates of anticipated

---

[8] See footnote [6] on page 26 for a discussion of proposed new terminology.
[9] *Ibid.*
[10] *Ibid.*

retirement. The past service cost is the amount of a theoretical pension fund which would have been in existence at the date of inception of the plan had the assumption as to entry ages been true. Under this method, annual normal cost tends to be level in amount.

The *individual level premium method*[11] assigns the cost of each employee's pension in level annual amounts over the period from the date of the employee's entry into the plan (for a new plan, the inception date) to his retirement. In applying this method, past service cost is not separately determined. Use of this method results in annual payments which at the outset are very high and which decline sharply from year to year as the employees initially covered retire and are replaced by younger employees.

The *aggregate method*[12] applies on a collective basis the principle followed for individuals in the individual level premium method. That is, the entire unfunded cost of future pension benefits, as of the date of an actuarial determination, is spread over the average future working lives of active employees. Under this method the annual payments decline, but more moderately than under the individual level premium method. The aggregate method may be modified by introducing past service cost, in which case the annual normal cost declines. If the past service cost is determined by the unit credit method, the procedure is called the *attained age normal method.*[13]

## Unrealized Appreciation (Depreciation) of Pension Fund Investments

In some actuarial cost calculations, the amount of the pension fund at the date of an actuarial determination directly affects the estimate of pension cost. In any event, the method of determining the amount of the fund may influence the actuarial assumption as to fund earnings (interest). Always, it is necessary to consider whether to recognize unrealized appreciation or depreciation of securities and other investments. Practice varies.

## FEDERAL INCOME TAX CONSEQUENCES

The Federal income tax consequences of a pension plan depend on whether the plan is a *qualified* one—that is, whether it complies with

---

[11] See footnote [6] on page 26 for a discussion of proposed new terminology.
[12] *Ibid.*
[13] *Ibid.*

certain requirements of the Internal Revenue Code and of the Internal Revenue Service. Pension plans in effect today have for the most part been designed to meet these requirements, since significant advantages attach to a qualified plan. (The principal exception is for plans operated on the pay-as-you-go basis; under such plans the making of tax-deductible payments by the employer coincides with the receipt of taxable benefits by retired employees.)[14]

## Deductibility of Contributions

As a general rule, the amounts an employer contributes under a qualified plan are deductible, subject to certain limitations, in the Federal income tax return for the year in which contributed. In the case of a taxpayer on the accrual basis, contributions accrued within a taxable year are deemed to have been paid on the last day of the taxable year if paid not later than the time prescribed by law for filing the return, including extensions.

The amount an employer may deduct in a taxable year for contributions under a qualified pension plan is subject to three general limitations, the least restrictive applying:

> Pension trust contributions may not exceed the amount reasonably necessary to fund the cost of the plan. Initially, the limitation deriving from this provision is 5 per cent of the total annual compensation otherwise paid or accrued to all employees participating in the plan. In the second year and at not less than five-year intervals thereafter, the Commissioner of Internal Revenue may recompute the amount of this limitation.
>
> Notwithstanding the limitation previously described, an amount necessary to provide the unfunded cost of the participants' past and current service credits, distributed as a level amount or a level percentage of compensation over the remaining future service of each participant, is deductible. (If, however, the unfunded cost for any three individuals is more than 50 per cent of the total unfunded cost, the unfunded cost attributable to those three individuals must be spread over a period of at least five taxable years.)
>
> Notwithstanding either of the limitations previously described, a taxpayer may deduct each year the total of (a) the normal cost of the plan and (b) 10 per cent of the initial past service cost (including any amount paid for interest). If a plan is substantially

---

[14] The requirements for qualification and the resulting advantages are discussed in Appendix A (page 102).

amended to provide increased prior service credits, a separate 10 per cent limitation applies to the additional funding from the time of amendment.

If the amount of contributions paid under a pension plan in any year exceeds the maximum amount deductible, the excess may be carried over and deducted in later years, subject to the limitations described.

In addition to the foregoing limitations, which operate to determine the maximum amounts the employer may deduct, there is a requirement that the unfunded prior service cost at any time not exceed the initial past service cost, except to the extent that any excess results from an amendment to the plan increasing benefits. In the event such an excess does arise, the Internal Revenue Service may challenge the qualified status of the plan. The requirement is met if the employer pays annually or cumulatively an amount equal to the normal cost plus interest, at the rate used in determining the present value of future benefit payments under the plan, on the amount of any unfunded balance of actuarially accrued cost at the beginning of the taxable year.

## Actuarial Cost Methods

The applicable regulations do not specify an actuarial cost method to be used in determining the employer's payments to pension trusts. The regulations provide in substance, however, that a taxpayer's choice of method for determining the amount deductible is binding for a taxable year for which the tax return has been filed. For subsequent years, the taxpayer is free to change to any other proper method without prior approval.

## Actuarial Assumptions

The regulations provide that the actuarial assumptions used in determining amounts paid to pension trusts should be consistent with reasonable expectation as to average experience and should not be so conservative as to anticipate the most unfavorable experience likely to occur. Although the Internal Revenue Service ordinarily does not specify the assumptions to be followed, one ruling[15] has set forth the conditions under which the interest rate assumed should not be less than 3.5 per cent.

---

[15] Revenue Ruling 63-11, January 1963.

# 3

# Timing the Charges to Expense

The central problems of this study are (1) whether generally accepted accounting principles should require accrual accounting for pension cost, (2) if so, how the accrual basis should be applied and (3) the nature and extent of the information about pension plans and pension cost which should appear in the employer's financial statements. This chapter will deal with the first two questions; Chapter 4 will deal with the third. Both chapters consider various possible solutions, expose the arguments and reach conclusions.

## UNDERLYING CONCEPTS

Certain elements of the environment in which the problems of accounting for pension cost must be resolved were discussed in Chapter 2. An equally important element of the environment is the entire fabric of accounting principles, including those fundamental concepts in which accounting is rooted. This study on pension cost accounting is part of a broad research program being conducted under the auspices of the American Institute of Certified Public Accountants through its Accounting Research Division and its Accounting Principles Board. Other phases of the program seek to establish the fundamental concepts (sometimes referred to as "postulates" and "principles") on which solutions to specific accounting problems, including the problems of accounting for the cost of pension plans, may be based.[1] Pending authoritative definition of the fundamental concepts underlying accounting procedures, it has been necessary to select some yardsticks against which the procedures considered in this study may be measured. The following concepts, widely agreed upon at present, have been chosen:

> *The going concern concept.* In the absence of evidence to the contrary, it is assumed that a business entity will remain in operation indefinitely (but not necessarily in perpetuity).
>
> *The matching concept.* The expenses to be charged against income in a particular accounting period are those which are incurred in producing, or which are otherwise reasonably related to, the revenues taken into income in the period.
>
> *The consistency concept.* Substantially identical transactions entered into by a particular company from time to time under substantially identical conditions are recorded in the same way. In practice, because of the complexities of business, transactions may differ from previous ones of similar purpose, and the surrounding conditions may vary. Consequently, the consistency concept does not mean that a company is expected to record the same amounts in succeeding periods for, say, depreciation or the cost of a pension plan. It does mean, however, that any variation should reflect differences in facts or differences in judgment—not differences in accounting principles or in the methods or practices followed in determining the amounts.

## SIMPLIFYING THE DISCUSSION

To simplify the discussion, three types of pension plans are set aside for later consideration: (1) plans in which the funding instrument consists of individual annuity or insurance policies or a group contract or contracts, (2) defined-contribution plans (those in which the em-

---

[1] Inquiries into the nature of accounting fundamentals have resulted in publication of: Maurice Moonitz, *Accounting Research Study No. 1*, "The Basic Postulates of Accounting," 1961; Robert T. Sprouse and Maurice Moonitz, *Accounting Research Study No. 3*, "A Tentative Set of Broad Accounting Principles for Business Enterprises," 1962; Paul Grady, *Accounting Research Study No. 7*, "Inventory of Generally Accepted Accounting Principles for Business Enterprises," 1965.

ployer's contributions are calculated by a stated formula—for example, a fixed amount for each ton produced or for each hour worked, or a fixed percentage of compensation) and (3) unfunded plans. Thus, the sections immediately following relate to defined-benefit plans in which the funding instrument is a trust agreement or a deposit administration contract or similar arrangement.

## CHOICE OF BASIS OF ACCOUNTING

The first facet of the problem to be considered in detail is whether generally accepted accounting principles should require that the *accrual basis* of accounting be used in assigning the cost of a pension plan to fiscal periods. The accrual basis is "the method of accounting whereby revenue and expense are identified with specific periods of time ... and are reported as *incurred* ..., without regard to the date of payment."[2] (By contrast, under the cash basis, "revenue and expense are recorded on the books of account when received and paid, respectively, without regard to the period to which they apply.")[3] Applied to pension cost, the accrual method would base periodic charges to expense (a) on one or more of the fundamental concepts described earlier in this chapter, rather than on the amounts paid and (b) on the substance of a pension plan rather than on its form. Arguments concerning the propriety of a requirement that the accrual basis be used for pension cost are presented in relation to two propositions.

PROPOSITION A. *The amount which should be recorded as the pension expense for a given accounting period is the amount paid for the period.*

ARGUMENTS IN FAVOR OF PROPOSITION A (ARGUMENTS IN FAVOR OF THE CASH BASIS)

• Flexibility is an important objective in accounting for the cost of pension plans. Hence, the amount *paid* for pensions is the appropriate measure of pension expense.

---

[2] Eric L. Kohler, *A Dictionary for Accountants*, Third Edition, 1963, p. 18.
[3] Kohler, *op. cit.*, p. 88.

- Financial (funding) policies as to pensions vary among companies. Accounting concepts that do not recognize such variations distort the true conditions.
- Because of the uncertainties involved (for example, mortality, employee turnover, pension fund earnings, the possibility that relocation of operations will relieve the employer of some or all of the pension obligations), any determination of the present cost of future pensions is an estimate, unsuitable for use in accounting provisions.
- Many employers, on competent advice, believe they will never be called upon to pay the entire amount of an actuarially calculated pension accrual. It is improper to make an accounting provision for amounts which will never be paid; such amounts are not true costs.
- Even if pension cost is accounted for by a method that disregards the amounts paid, uniformity in pension accounting will not result. So many elements of judgment enter into the calculations an actuary makes in determining pension cost, and the field of acceptable alternative practices for actuaries is so wide, that comparability is not a practical possibility.
- The manner and extent of funding (paying) pension cost will influence recorded pension expense in spite of an intent to the contrary, because funding directly affects fund earnings which in turn ultimately affect the amount of pension cost.
- Accruing pension cost without setting aside funds does not effectively extinguish the liability for pensions; the funds remain at risk in the business in the same way as though no accrual had been made.
- Changing the present accounting procedures for pension cost might have serious adverse consequences, among which are the following: (1) *Misunderstanding*. If accounting provisions for pension cost were to differ from amounts funded, large liabilities or deferred charges might appear in employers' balance sheets. These items would be confusing to both stockholders and employees. (2) *Additional funding*. If liabilities were to appear, employee organizations might be encouraged to demand additional funding. Even in the absence of such pressure, some employers might choose to fund on the basis of the accounting charges. Additional funding, for whatever reason undertaken, might place an unnecessary financial burden on the employer to the detriment of both stockholders and employees. As a further undesirable consequence of additional funding, the amount of financial resources (and, hence, economic power) concentrated in pension funds would be increased. (3) *Liabilities*. Upon termination of a pension plan, amounts shown as liabilities might be held payable to employees even though the employer is not otherwise legally obligated to make further pay-

ments. Liabilities recorded for pension cost might raise questions under loan agreements whose provisions limit additional borrowing or the payment of dividends. Such liabilities might also have significance in determining whether a corporate dividend causes an impairment of capital. (4) *Limitation of benefits.* A requirement having the effect of increasing employers' charges for pension expense might significantly limit the level of pension benefits which employers will undertake to provide, either through new plans or by improving existing plans.

• To account for pension cost on a basis different from the funding basis would burden employers with additional expense, including actuaries' fees for separate actuarial valuations for accounting purposes.

ARGUMENTS AGAINST PROPOSITION A (ARGUMENTS IN FAVOR OF THE ACCRUAL BASIS)

• Pension plans, in practical effect, are part of compensation. In almost all cases, one of the employer's principal reasons for adopting a pension plan is to make it easier to obtain and retain employees of high competence. In wage negotiations, labor unions frequently accept additional pension benefits in lieu of all or part of a proposed increase in current wages. Consequently, employers should account for pension cost when incurred (not when paid).

• Even if pensions are held not to be part of *compensation,* the cost of providing them is nevertheless an *employment cost* which should be accounted for when incurred.

• The amount paid for pensions for a given period may by coincidence or design equal an accounting charge determined on the accrual basis, but the amount paid is not *per se* a proper determinant of the accounting charge.

• The cost of pension benefits to be paid in the future is a continuing present expense of the employer. An allowance for such cost is one of the expenses to be matched with the employer's revenues for an accounting period.

• If flexibility in accounting for pension cost means the absence of undue rigidity, flexibility is a desirable objective. If, however, flexibility means license to charge to operations any amount which may be convenient, then flexibility is undesirable.

• The extent of pension funding in a fiscal period is a matter of management decision entirely unrelated to accounting considerations. Hence, charging payments (rather than amounts determined on the accrual basis) to expense may impair the significance of net income, both for a single employer (between years) and among employers.

- Accounting provisions for pension cost should be rationally and consistently determined. Accounting provisions based on the amounts paid, however, may vary with profits or be influenced by other inappropriate considerations. Employers may properly *contribute* more to pension trusts in good years and less, or nothing at all, in lean years. It does not follow, however, that the *accounting* provisions should vary correspondingly.
- To be sure, significant uncertainties must be resolved in estimating pension cost. But uncertainties must be resolved in many accounting determinations. Actuaries can make estimates of such cost which are sufficiently accurate for accounting purposes.
- To argue that full *funding* of pension cost may be unnecessary, and that it is therefore inappropriate to *accrue* the cost, is to advocate borrowing from Peter to pay Paul. It is similar to suggesting that the full amount of accounts payable need not be recorded because the *aggregate amount* of accounts payable is unlikely ever to be reduced below a certain level (a proposition which no one supports). If the aggregate of accounts payable is not reduced, it is because amounts owing to specific suppliers are continually being replaced by amounts owing to other suppliers. If full funding of pension cost is unnecessary, it is because the amounts the employer contributes are not identified with specific employees. Thus, amounts contributed in recognition of the current service of present employees may be used to pay pensions to former employees who have retired. If the employer's business is to continue (as the going concern concept assumes), the cost of providing pensions for present employees must eventually be met and so should be recognized in expense currently.
- It is true that variations in pension charges may result from differences in (1) judgment in resolving uncertainties as to future events, (2) actuarial methods and (3) the extent of funding. On the other hand, the possibility—or even the likelihood—that such variations will occur is not a valid argument for a condition in which the sole criterion for determining the accounting charge for pension cost is the amount of a payment arbitrarily determined by the employer.
- The indirect consequences of accrual accounting for pension cost cannot be accurately foretold; the possibly adverse impact of such accounting on the economy of the nation or on the affairs of individual employers, foreseen by those who advocate charge-what-you-pay accounting for pensions, is conjectural. The consequences of ignoring part of the cost of pension commitments may be equally adverse, both

for the economy and for individual companies. The problems which may arise because unfunded pension expense is shown in the liability section of the employer's balance sheet may be overcome, at least in part, by choosing a balance sheet caption which clearly identifies the amount (for example, "Excess of pension expense over payments").

• To be sure, accounting for pension cost on a basis different from the funding basis may be expected to create some additional out-of-pocket expense. This would not, however, be as great as some suggest. A separate, complete actuarial valuation would not be required, since many of the procedures undertaken in a valuation for funding purposes could be adapted to obtain amounts for accounting purposes.

PROPOSITION B. *There should not be an accounting requirement which would lead an employer to record expense under a pension plan in an amount exceeding the legal responsibility imposed by the plan.*

ARGUMENTS IN FAVOR OF PROPOSITION B (ARGUMENTS IN FAVOR OF THE LEGAL LIABILITY VIEW)

• A pension plan is a contract; except in rare cases its terms carefully define the employer's responsibilities. In some plans, for example, the employer is responsible only to the extent of payments; in others, employees' vested rights are a determining factor. Any payments exceeding the legal responsibility are discretionary. To require accounting provisions in excess of payments which fulfill the requirements of a plan would be to sweep aside the legal realities and would thus be unjustified.

• Accruals in some cases might impair a company's ability to pay dividends or might result in defaults under indentures or other agreements. If the company otherwise has met its obligations under its pension plan, such a result is unwarranted.

• Using the accrual basis for pension cost is quite different from providing in the accounts for liabilities which are unquestioned but of which the amounts are conjectural. The pension cost to be recorded is the real cost (that is, the cash payments based upon the legal liabilities), rather than hypothetical amounts based upon assumptions not founded on fact.

ARGUMENTS AGAINST PROPOSITION B (ARGUMENTS AGAINST THE LEGAL LIABILITY VIEW)

- Accounting for the cost of pension plans should be based upon the substance of the employer's situation. Experience shows that pension plans, once adopted, become in practical effect a permanent part of the employer's compensation structure. Plans subject to specific termination dates are renewed regularly. In the ordinary course of events, plans which give the employer a right of termination are not terminated but are continued in force indefinitely. Vesting provisions act to determine the employer's minimum pension cost on a liquidation basis, not the cost incurred on a going concern basis. In the absence of convincing evidence that legal limitations on the employer's liability will take effect, they should not be dominant in determining accounting provisions for pension cost.
- It is true that, if accrual accounting is adopted for pension plans, there may be instances in which contractual limitations on an employer's pension liability, not recognized in accounting for the cost of a plan, take effect later. Such limitations may take effect, for example, if the employer discontinues all or part of its business, is adjudged bankrupt or moves a plant. Compared with the number of employers having pension plans, the number for whom such eventualities may be expected to affect pension commitments significantly is small. The possibility that a few companies may be required to adjust their pension accounts upon the occurrence of unforeseen events is not a valid argument against an accounting procedure that is otherwise sound.

CONCLUSION ON CHOICE OF BASIS OF ACCOUNTING

*It is a conclusion of this study that an employer's financial position and results of operations, to the extent affected by the cost of a pension plan, are fairly presented only if such cost is stated on the accrual basis.*

If the cash basis is used, the employer's charges for pension expense may reflect the influence of factors not properly considered in a sound determination of financial position and results of operations—for example, the availability of cash or the level of the employer's earnings before deducting pension cost. In some years, employers using the cash basis may record a reduced amount of pension expense because the payment is reduced, or they may record no expense because there is no payment.

It is true that many companies which recognize pension cost on the cash basis are, by coincidence or intent, also complying with the accrual basis. That is, the payments they make for pensions are determined on a basis which meets accrual accounting criteria. But in the absence of a requirement for accrual accounting, even those companies which coincidentally follow the accrual basis may revert to cash basis accounting if conditions arise which make the accrual basis inconvenient.

Accrual accounting for the cost of pension plans draws support from the analysis of viewpoints presented in this section and from each of the fundamental concepts discussed at the beginning of this chapter.

Under the *going concern concept,* accounting assumes that an employer will continue in business indefinitely. Experience shows that in most instances a pension plan, once adopted, also continues indefinitely. By and large, this holds true despite the presence of clauses which may limit either (a) the rights of employees or their representatives to enforce claims against the employer or (b) the amounts of such claims. Termination provisions and other provisions limiting the liability of the employer are ordinarily not invoked if the employer continues as a going concern. Consequently, it is proper to proceed, in the absence of convincing contrary evidence, on the assumption that the employer will continue to provide the pension benefits called for in the present plan or plans.

Under the *matching concept,* the expenses to be assigned to an accounting period should include an allowance for the continuing present cost of future pension benefits. The cost of such benefits is a business expense which is related to the present work force and is a function of the passage of time—including time in the present period. This expense continues whether or not payments are made for pension cost, and the amount of the expense properly related to a given period is not contingent on the amount paid.

Under the *consistency concept,* the amounts charged to expense from time to time should be determined in the same way and should not be subject either to arbitrary variation or to the influence of factors not properly considered in a sound determination of financial position and results of operations.

## APPLYING THE ACCRUAL BASIS

A recommendation for accrual accounting does not of itself provide sufficient guidance for determining the amount and timing of an employer's charges to expense for pension cost, since a number of significant questions arise in applying the accrual basis. The first is: What cost must be accounted for? Opposing views are embodied in the following antithetic descriptions of an acceptable minimum annual charge for expense under a pension plan:

> An appropriately assigned portion of the cost (present value) of *specific pension benefits* expected to become payable in the future to *specific persons*.
>
> versus
>
> An amount such that, if similarly determined amounts were contributed annually to a fund, *the plan* would be enabled to remain in operation indefinitely.

The practical significance of the difference in viewpoints will become manifest as the discussion turns to (a) *actuarial cost methods,* which are used in calculating pension cost, and (b) *normal cost* and *past service cost,* of which pension cost is composed.

## 40  Actuarial Cost Methods[4]

Another important question in applying the accrual basis concerns the extent to which the several actuarial cost methods by which pension cost may be assigned to periods of time are acceptable for use in accrual accounting. The methods under consideration are those used at present[5] in determining employers' payments which are charged to expense.

Two of the procedures sometimes used in determining the amounts of employers' payments under pension plans are so clearly unsuitable for accrual accounting that it seems pointless to present arguments supporting their use. The *pay-as-you-go* procedure is unacceptable be-

---

[4] Actuarial cost methods are discussed in Appendix C (page 121). Because their primary use in the past has been in determining amounts to be paid, actuarial cost methods are referred to in Appendix C as "funding methods." See footnote [6] on page 26 for a discussion of proposed new terminology.

[5] In limiting the discussion to methods presently in use, it is not intended to reject without study other methods which may subsequently come into use. As an example of consideration which has been given to the development of other actuarial cost methods, see Charles L. Trowbridge, "The Unfunded Present Value Family of Pension Funding Methods," *Transactions of the Society of Actuaries,* Volume XV, 1963, pp. 151-192.

cause it records pension cost only when retirement benefits are paid. The *terminal funding method* must also be rejected because it recognizes pension cost only at the end of an employee's period of active service. Neither procedure is considered to be an "actuarial cost method."

Differences of opinion about the acceptability for accounting purposes of the several actuarial methods center around such questions as whether employers should have flexibility in choice of method and whether the results produced by certain of the methods are reasonable. Viewpoints are presented in relation to the following proposition.

PROPOSITION C. *The* entry age normal method *is the only actuarial cost method acceptable for use in accounting for pension cost on the accrual basis.*

ARGUMENTS IN FAVOR OF PROPOSITION C (ARGUMENTS AGAINST FLEXIBILITY IN CHOICE OF ACTUARIAL COST METHOD)

- In order to insure uniformity among employers in accounting for pension cost, a single actuarial cost method must be selected.
- If past service cost is accrued in level annual amounts, the entry age normal method produces the most reasonable aggregate annual charge for pension cost. Under this method, the annual normal cost is either a level amount or a level percentage of the compensation of covered employees. In practice, under this method, variations in annual pension expense may occur, but only as a result of factors such as actuarial gains and losses, changes in pension benefits, fluctuations in employment levels or employee distribution, and the effects of accounting for past service cost.
- The other actuarial cost methods customarily used in funding pension plans are not acceptable for accrual accounting because the annual pension charges they produce are not level (either absolutely or as a percentage of payroll) but tend to increase or decrease annually, at least for a relatively long period of time. For an immature employee group (which is typical), the normal cost under the *unit credit method* increases annually. (The increase may, however, be camouflaged by the effects of other factors.) Under both the *individual level premium method* and the *aggregate method,* which include past service cost and current service cost in a single amount, the periodic charge starts at a relatively high level and decreases annually over a comparatively long

period of time (the downtrend in the *aggregate method* is less severe but is none the less significant). Under the *attained age normal method,* there is a downtrend in normal cost.[6]

ARGUMENTS AGAINST PROPOSITION C (ARGUMENTS IN FAVOR OF FLEXIBILITY IN CHOICE OF ACTUARIAL COST METHOD)

- Any rational method of allocating total pension cost to periods of time should be acceptable if it is applied in a reasonable manner and is followed consistently.
- Levelness in annual charges, either in the absolute or as a percentage of compensation, is not a valid objective in accounting for pension cost. Such an objective is not inherent in the accrual basis.
- Each of the actuarial cost methods relies on arbitrary assumptions (not the so-called "actuarial assumptions") as to the incidence of pension cost. For example, the unit credit method assumes that pension cost accrues (in the accounting sense) as benefits accrue (in the limited sense that the units of employee service on which benefits are based have been rendered); the entry age normal method assumes (1) that each employee entered the plan at the time of employment or at the earliest time he would have been eligible if the plan had then been in existence and (2) that contributions (accruals) have been made on this basis from the entry age to the date of the actuarial valuation (the contributions—accruals—are level annual amounts which, if paid into a fund and accumulated at the interest rate used in the actuarial valuation, would at the time of the employee's retirement equal the then present value of his pension). Because the assumptions are arbitrary, it is not possible to single out one of the actuarial cost methods which alone accomplishes a reasonable assignment of pension cost among accounting periods.
- The impracticality of prescribing a single actuarial method is demonstrated by the number of plans covering very small groups. For practical reasons the funding instrument under such plans usually consists of individual annuity or insurance contracts, which ordinarily use the individual level premium method. The premiums under that method are quite different from costs computed on the entry age normal method.
- Narrow requirements for uniform accounting treatment would re-

---

[6] For a comparison of the results of various actuarial cost methods in a hypothetical situation, see Table I, Appendix C (pages 124-125).

strict the development of the pension movement and might cause employers to discontinue existing plans.

* The range in available actuarial methods may be likened to the range in available methods for determining the cost of inventories or determining depreciation. As to inventories, for example, management may choose the last-in-first-out method, the first-in-first-out method or the average method; for depreciation, management may choose either the straight line method or an "accelerated" method such as the double-declining-balance method. For so long as management has such latitude in these and other areas, management ought also to have wide latitude in selecting an actuarial method for use in accruing pension cost.

* In addition to the entry age normal method, other actuarial cost methods, if applied consistently, result in systematic and rational charges to periodic income and meet the requirements of accrual accounting.

CONCLUSION ON ACTUARIAL COST METHODS

*It is a conclusion of this study that the actuarial cost methods presently used in calculating payments under pension plans are acceptable for use in accrual accounting if they are applied in accordance with the other conclusions of the study.* (*Pay-as-you-go* and *terminal funding* are unacceptable because they do not make provision for the cost of future retirement benefits during employees' periods of active service. They are not exceptions to the conclusion stated, however, because they are not considered to be actuarial cost methods.)

Because of the long-range nature of pension commitments and the extent of the uncertainties involved in estimating pension cost, this study prefers that pension expense be recorded as nearly as possible in level annual amounts, varied only to give effect to changes in facts. (Examples of the latter are variations in the level of employment, increases in pension benefits resulting from a plan amendment, and the effects of accounting for past service cost.) The actuarial cost method which most nearly accomplishes this objective is the entry age normal method, which is, therefore, preferred.

## Normal Cost

*It is a conclusion of this study that provision should be made annually for the normal cost of a pension plan*—the cost assigned, under the actuarial cost method used, to years subsequent to the inception of the plan.

This conclusion is supported by the fundamental concepts discussed at the beginning of this chapter and by the arguments presented favoring accrual accounting for pension cost. Without significant exception, those who favor such accounting will endorse the conclusion stated. This may be, however, the only aspect of pension cost accounting on which there is anything approaching unanimity, and it must be emphasized that even this consensus exists only among those who accept the accrual basis.

## Past Service Cost

If there is limited agreement on accounting for normal cost, there is extensive disagreement on accounting for past service cost—the cost assigned, under the actuarial cost method used, to years prior to the inception of a pension plan. A few would charge past service cost retroactively to the prior years. Others would charge such cost to expense in subsequent years, but only to the extent funded (including amounts identified as "interest"). Still others would bring such cost (and related charges for interest) into expense over a "reasonable period" following the inception of a pension plan. Those in this last group disagree as to the duration of the period in which an employer realizes the advantages associated with the past service element of a pension plan. Some in this group associate the employer's advantages with the remaining service lives of employees initially covered. Others believe the advantages are so nebulous that the employer should have wide latitude in selecting an accrual period. Proposals identifying the period range from a relatively short time—for example, ten years or the period of between eleven and twelve years which results from applying the Federal income tax rule limiting the annual deduction for past service cost to (generally) 10 per cent of the initial amount—to an indefinitely long time. If the period chosen is so long that it approaches infinity, the past service cost is not accrued at all, and only interest on the initial amount is charged. Among those who would limit accruals for past service cost to amounts equal to interest are those holding the view that the annual charge for pension expense should be the amount necessary to enable the plan to remain in operation (page 40). For many plans, an annual contribution comprising the normal cost and interest on the unfunded past service cost accomplishes this purpose.

In the discussion following, viewpoints on accounting for past service cost are presented in relation to four of many possible procedures, assuming that in any event each year's expense is to include the normal cost (determined, in the first three procedures, by the same actuarial cost method used to determine the past service cost).

PROPOSITION D. *Past service cost should be charged to retained earnings at the inception of a pension plan.*

ARGUMENTS IN FAVOR OF PROPOSITION D (ARGUMENTS IN FAVOR OF A CHARGE TO PRIOR YEARS)

• If a plan giving pension credits to employees for years prior to its adoption had been in effect in such years, provision would have been made for the related cost. The charge to retained earnings is, in effect, a retroactive adjustment of the income statements for such prior years.

• It is illogical to burden current periods with cost relating to past service if charges are also being made for the normal cost under an accepted method of calculation.

• This procedure would eliminate lack of comparability among companies resulting from the use of different methods of accounting for past service cost. It would also overcome any lack of comparability between periods for a single company resulting from differences in amounts of past service cost charged to different periods (for example, when accrual is completed).

• If two men working side by side turn out the same number of units of the same product, the cost should not differ merely because one of the employees is older (and more past service cost is consequently assigned to his production).

ARGUMENTS AGAINST PROPOSITION D (ARGUMENTS AGAINST A CHARGE TO PRIOR YEARS)

• Employers adopt pension plans because they expect to realize present and future advantages. For example, one of the usual purposes of adopting a pension plan is to encourage older employees to retire, thus improving operating efficiency. Another common purpose is to help the employer attract and hold competent employees. Past service cost is part of the cost of obtaining such advantages. Consequently, past service cost should be charged to those present and future periods during which the advantages are expected to be realized, not, in effect, to periods prior to the inception of the plan.

• Acknowledging comparability in financial statements (or uniformity in accounting) as an objective does not validate charging past service cost to retained earnings. Such cost is applicable to periods after the inception of the plan.

- The fact that the benefits under a plan are *measured* by past service does not necessarily mean that their cost applies to the periods during which such service was rendered.
- The argument about employees working side by side and producing identical quantities of the same item fails because it sets up an arbitrary presumption that the employment cost for the two individuals *should* be the same. In point of fact, there may be numerous differentials in employment cost, of which the variation in the element of past service cost is only one example.

PROPOSITION E. *Past service cost should be charged to expense only to the extent funded (including amounts identified as "interest").*

ARGUMENTS IN FAVOR OF PROPOSITION E (ARGUMENTS AGAINST ACCRUAL OF PAST SERVICE COST)

- Many employers, on competent advice, believe they will never be called upon to fund past service cost, except to the extent of interest (to keep the unfunded cost from growing). It is unnecessary and improper to make an accounting provision for amounts which will never be paid; such amounts are not true cost. A company may decide to fund past service cost as a voluntary act of conservatism beyond the requirements of its plan, but this does not prove that the company must provide in its accounts for past service cost not funded.
- In granting past service credits under a pension plan, an employer obtains diverse advantages of indefinite duration. Past service cost is thus in the nature of an intangible which does not diminish in value and which need not be amortized (accrued).
- To require an annual provision for past service cost (exceeding payments) is to espouse an erroneous concept—that pension accounting can be based on particular people at a particular time. Actuarial assumptions are not valid for individuals. Rather, the assumptions are a function of a mass of employees such as those moving through the plan over the years. Accordingly, contributions (and accruals) are not made with respect to specific individuals; instead, they apply to the entire group of employees, the aggregate of those covered.

- If past service cost is accrued but not funded, the resulting balance sheet credit is difficult to justify. If a liability, it is a curious one, since it is not payable to anyone in particular.
- If levelness of accounting charges for pension cost is desired, accruing past service cost is to be avoided, since a sharp drop in annual pension expense may occur when accrual of past service cost has been completed.
- If charges to expense for past service cost exceed the amounts funded, there may be serious indirect adverse consequences. These consequences were cited earlier in this chapter (page 34) in discussing accrual accounting for pension cost.
- Pension cost is a loading on employment cost, but without regard to the way employees' benefits are measured and without regard to any particular period of time, either before or after the adoption of a pension plan. The key requirement is that the annual pension charge be a reasonable measurement of the annual amount required to balance the benefits to be paid in the future. This requirement is satisfied by a perpetuity whose present value is equal to the present value of the aggregate of the potential benefits to all *present and future* employees under the plan. For a relatively mature employee group, the amount of such an annuity would be approximately the same as an annual contribution of normal cost plus interest on past service cost for *present* employees, determined under either the unit credit method or the entry age normal method.
- Many companies, in successful years, pay discretionary additional compensation (bonuses). Other companies have deferred profit-sharing arrangements (for many companies, the sole vehicle used to provide retirement benefits). The cost of both bonuses and profit-sharing plans varies from year to year. Consequently, employers should have flexibility in deciding when (if at all) to charge past service cost to expense.

ARGUMENTS AGAINST PROPOSITION E (ARGUMENTS IN FAVOR OF ACCRUAL OF PAST SERVICE COST)

- As pointed out in an argument against Proposition D, past service cost is a cost of providing pensions for the employees initially covered and so should be charged to expense over a reasonable period following the inception of a plan.
- The proposal to limit the annual accrual for past service cost to an amount identified as interest (unless more is funded) requires cautious analysis. The significance of interest in estimating pension cost is two-

fold: First, the pension benefits whose cost is to be recorded currently will be paid at varying times in the future; consequently, the cost is expressed in terms of the present value of the benefits expected to be paid. Second, there is an expectation that earnings on pension fund investments will provide part of the money needed to pay benefits; the anticipated rate of earnings is used in calculating the present value of future benefits. Because pension cost is stated at present value, any amount assigned to present or prior periods, but not funded, increases in each succeeding year by the amount of interest unless an amount equivalent to interest is paid. Under regulations of the Internal Revenue Service, the qualified status of a pension plan may be challenged if the unfunded prior service cost at any time exceeds the initial unfunded amount. Consequently, many employers having trust fund plans contribute annually (or cumulatively) amounts equal to the normal cost plus interest on any unfunded prior service cost, including past service cost. Accounting provisions based on such contributions are not a satisfactory substitute for accruing the past service cost itself, since such provisions merely recognize increments in unfunded prior service cost (interest) resulting from the passage of time.

- It is specious to contend (as one of the arguments favoring Proposition E contends) that individuals have no significance in accounting for pension cost. Facts concerning individuals are the raw materials of the calculation; the purpose is to estimate the cost of providing pensions for a specific group of individuals.
- If full *funding* of past service cost appears unnecessary, it is precisely because fund assets are not identified with specific employees. For example, amounts contributed as interest on past service cost or in recognition of current service may be used to pay pensions to former employees who have retired. Nevertheless, if the employer's business is to continue (as the going concern concept assumes), the total cost of providing pensions for present employees, including the past service cost, must eventually be met and so should be recognized in expense.
- It is true that the specific persons to whom past service cost is payable are not identified in the employer's accounts. The persons for whom pension cost is accrued are identified, however, in the supporting calculations. Further, there is ample precedent for accruing estimated liabilities not immediately payable to specific creditors. An example is a provision for the cost of repairing products sold under a warranty.
- The *accounting* requirement to recognize past service cost over the period benefited by the past service element of the plan is independent of the employer's decision to fund (or not to fund) such cost.

This accounting requirement arises from the concept of matching the appropriate expenses (including past service pension cost) with the revenues of an accounting period.

- Levelness in the accounting charges for pension cost over an extended period has, indeed, been recognized as desirable. A desire to achieve such a condition, however, is not an adequate reason for failing to record an element of cost.
- There may, indeed, be indirect adverse consequences if past service cost is accrued but not funded. These consequences cannot accurately be foretold. In any event, ignoring part of the cost of pension commitments may have equally serious adverse effects.
- The proposal to base the annual pension accrual on the amount of an annuity for both *present and future* employees is an interesting exercise in mathematics; it is not relevant, however, to the problem of accounting for the cost of providing pensions for *present* employees.
- An employer's commitments under a pension plan are long-term, and do not vary from year to year as do commitments under bonus arrangements or profit-sharing plans. The cost of providing pension benefits is independent of the employer's earnings and so should be recognized regularly without regard to earnings.

PROPOSITION F. *Past service cost should be charged in equal annual amounts (including "interest") over the average remaining service life, from the inception of the plan, of employees initially covered.*

ARGUMENTS IN FAVOR OF PROPOSITION F (ARGUMENTS IN FAVOR OF ACCRUAL OVER AVERAGE REMAINING SERVICE LIFE)

- The arguments against Proposition E are, in turn, arguments favoring a regular annual charge for past service cost. Such a charge is an objective of Proposition F.
- A pension plan, once adopted, becomes part of the employer's compensation structure. Thus, the employees initially covered earn their pensions during the period from the inception of a plan to their retirement. Under this "earning concept," the employer should accrue the past service cost of the plan over that same period.
- Whether or not the "earning concept" is accepted, past service cost is part of the cost of providing pensions for the employees initially covered, and should be charged to expense over the remaining service lives of such employees.

- While it may be true that the period benefited by the past service element of a pension plan is indefinite in length, by far the greater part of the benefit is related to the service lives of the employees who will receive pensions measured in part by past service. Hence, past service cost should be charged to expense during the remaining period of service of such employees.

ARGUMENTS AGAINST PROPOSITION F (ARGUMENTS AGAINST ACCRUAL OVER AVERAGE REMAINING SERVICE LIFE)

- Pension cost is, to be sure, a business expense which is related to the aging of the work force. This does not mean, however, that the "earning concept" is appropriate. The advantages to an employer arising from the past service element of a pension plan extend over an indefinite period which cannot be identified with any degree of certainty.
- Accrual of past service cost on a diminishing charge basis should be acceptable, since the cost can logically be identified with *individual* remaining service lives, rather than with the *average* remaining service life. On the individual basis, the accrual would decrease annually as the employees to whom the past service cost applies retire. Diminishing annual amortization of past service cost is, in effect, achieved under the individual level premium method and the aggregate method, both of which are acceptable under a conclusion reached earlier in this chapter (page 43).
- Employers should have latitude in selecting an accrual period. At this stage in the development of accounting for the cost of pension plans, it is more important to secure recognition of the necessity for accruing past service cost than to insure uniformity in the choice of accrual period. This suggestion for latitude in selecting an accrual period for past service cost is compatible with the conclusion, reached earlier in this chapter (page 43), which affirmed latitude in selecting an actuarial cost method.

PROPOSITION G. *Regardless of the actuarial method used in determining the normal cost, further accounting charges for the principal of past service cost should not be required when the assets of the pension fund, at market value, and any pension liability on the employer's books are equal to or in excess of the value of "accrued benefits." (A modification of Proposition F.)*

ARGUMENTS IN FAVOR OF PROPOSITION G (ARGUMENTS IN FAVOR OF LIMITING PAST SERVICE CHARGES TO THE UNIT CREDIT AMOUNT)

- When a pension plan is terminated in whole or in part (for example, upon sale of a plant or upon cessation for some other reason of operations at a particular location), the applicable provisions of the plan control the allocation of any pension fund assets among the participants. Ordinarily, assets are allocated first to employees who have retired and to those eligible for retirement. Covered employees not eligible to retire may receive allocations based on vested benefits or on credited service. If the entry age normal method or one of the other "level-cost" methods has been used, or if there has been appreciation in fund assets which has not been recognized, the fund may exceed the amount necessary to provide the "accrued benefits," and the employer may not be able to recover the excess. Therefore, it is inadvisable for an employer to make further contributions toward unfunded past service cost when the assets of a pension fund (valued at market) and any pension liability shown by the employer's books, taken together, equal or exceed the value of "accrued benefits." If *payments* are to be limited in this manner, it is appropriate similarly to limit *accounting charges*.
- The value of "accrued benefits" under a pension plan can be measured only by the unit credit method. Nevertheless, the measurement of this value is independent of the actuarial cost method used for accounting (or funding) purposes. The measurement of past service cost, however, is dependent upon the actuarial cost method used for accounting (or funding) purposes. (The difference may be illustrated by reference to Table I of Appendix C, pages 124-125. The value of "accrued benefits" is initially $431,924. The past service cost is equal to the value of "accrued benefits" under the unit credit method but is a greater amount, $661,315, under the entry age normal method. At any subsequent determination date, a similar difference would exist between prior service cost and the value of "accrued benefits.") It is improper to require further accounting charges for past service cost when the value of "accrued benefits" has been fully accounted for (as described in Proposition G).
- If the entry age normal method (for example) has been used for accounting purposes up to the time when "accrued benefits" have been fully accounted for, subsequent accounting charges should thereafter be limited to an amount comprising the normal cost (determined by the entry age normal method) and interest on the unfunded past serv-

ice cost (determined by the entry age normal method). For most plans, an annual charge on this basis would approximate a charge equal to the normal cost under the unit credit method and would maintain the "fully accrued" status of the plan. Changing to the unit credit method, however, may be impractical in some instances. Many plans do not lend themselves to the calculation of a unit of benefit "accruing" each year so that the cost of such a unit can be determined. It is possible, by defining terms, to determine the value of "accrued benefits" at any date, but it is difficult in many cases to forecast the value of the unit of benefits which would be expected to accrue during the ensuing year, since the amount of the accrual would depend on the increase in average earnings as well as the increase in credited service.

ARGUMENTS AGAINST PROPOSITION G (ARGUMENTS AGAINST LIMITING PAST SERVICE CHARGES TO THE UNIT CREDIT AMOUNT)

• Without question, it is appropriate for an employer to limit *payments* to a pension fund in the manner described in Proposition G if the employer so desires. This does not necessarily mean, however, that a similar limitation on *accounting charges* is appropriate. Limiting charges for past service cost in the manner described would make the possibility of termination of a plan a controlling factor in accounting for the cost and so would violate the going concern concept.

• A principal difference between the unit credit method and the entry age normal method is that at any time the unit credit method will have accounted for less cost in the aggregate than will the entry age normal method (using the same actuarial assumptions). This difference is a consequence of a fundamental difference in the assumptions (as to the incidence of pension cost) underlying the two methods, as described below. The question raised by Proposition G is whether the value of "accrued benefits" (an amount determined under the unit credit method) has any controlling accounting significance. Limiting accounting charges for past service cost to the unit credit amount can be shown to be universally appropriate only if it can also be shown that pension cost is universally incurred according to the assumptions (as to the incidence of pension cost) on which unit credit calculations are based. But, if it is *ever* true that pension cost is incurred as determined by the unit credit method—and no other—it is true from the *inception* of every plan. The corollary, which this study rejects, is that only the unit credit method is acceptable—at any time—for accounting purposes.

• Each actuarial cost method relies on arbitrary assumptions (not

• the so-called "actuarial assumptions") as to the incidence of pension cost. For example, the unit credit method assumes that pension cost is incurred as benefits "accrue" (in the limited sense that the units of employee service on which benefits are based have been rendered); the entry age normal method assumes (1) that each employee entered the plan at the time of employment or at the earliest time he would have been eligible if the plan had then been in existence and (2) that accounting charges have been made on this basis from the entry age to the date of the actuarial valuation (the accounting charges are level annual amounts which, if paid into a fund and accumulated at the interest rate used in the valuation, would at the time of the employee's retirement equal the then present value of his pension). Because the assumptions are arbitrary, it is not possible to single out one of the actuarial cost methods which alone accomplishes a reasonable assignment of pension cost among accounting periods. Recognizing this, the study has concluded (page 43) that any of several actuarial cost methods is acceptable for use in accounting. On the other hand, the test proposed in Proposition G is solely a unit credit test. Consequently, if the proposal has merit, logic would require that a company using a method other than the unit credit method in the early years of a plan change to the unit credit method when the value of "accrued benefits" has been fully accounted for. This study has concluded that the unit credit method is acceptable for accounting purposes. Consequently, no objection would be raised should a company make such a change, provided the effect were properly disclosed.

• It is inconsistent to contend (as in Proposition G) that charges for past service cost should terminate at a time which is to be determined by applying a unit credit test and at the same time to contend that it is impractical to use the unit credit method in determining accounting charges. If it is possible to determine the value of "accrued benefits" at the beginning of a year, it should be possible to forecast the value as of the end of the year. Hence, it should be possible to use the unit credit method.

CONCLUSION ON PAST SERVICE COST

*It is a conclusion of this study that past service cost should be taken into expense (together with related charges for interest) systematically over a reasonable period following the inception of a pension plan.*

The study has dealt separately with past service cost only because some of the actuarial techniques commonly used determine this element of pension cost separately. The fact that an element of pension cost is *measured* by service prior to the inception of a plan, however, does not give rise to an accounting distinction between such cost and cost measured by future service. Employers adopt pension plans providing past service credits because they foresee present and future advantages. The cost related to past service, whether or not determined separately, should be charged to expense during the period to which such advantages apply.

In concluding that past service cost should be taken into expense over a reasonable period following the inception of a pension plan, the study answers the question raised earlier in this chapter (page 40): What cost must be accounted for? The study accepts the view that the cost to be accounted for is the cost of *specific pension benefits* expected to become payable to *specific persons;* it does not accept the concept that the cost to be recognized is limited to an amount necessary to keep *the plan* in operation. For many plans, annual contributions comprising the normal cost and (merely) interest on the unfunded past service cost accomplish this latter purpose.

For reasons given in the preceding analysis of accounting arguments (Proposition G, page 50), it is unsatisfactory, under an actuarial cost method other than the unit credit method, to terminate accounting charges for past service cost when the value of "accrued benefits" (determined under the unit credit method) has been fully accounted for. This study has concluded, however, that the unit credit method is acceptable for accounting purposes. Consequently, a company using another method may change to the unit credit method, thus accomplishing the objective of limiting charges for past service cost. Disclosure in the event of a change in actuarial cost method is discussed in Chapter 4 (page 88).

The advantages to an employer of granting past service pensions are diverse; this study has not brought to light criteria for identifying with certainty the period in which such advantages are realized. It seems clear, however, that in most instances the greater part of the advantage is related to the periods in which the employees who will receive pensions based on past service will complete their employment. Consequently, a weighted average of the remaining service lives of such employees should be a starting point in determining the accrual period. Because the period cannot be definitely identified, however, there should be flexibility. A reasonable range would seem to be from a minimum of ten years to a maximum of forty years. The minimum period of ten years is equal to the minimum for income tax purposes (if past service cost is paid in advance). Using a short period would make it easier for a company which expects to grant increased pension benefits, thus creating additional prior service cost, to approach the practical objective of maintaining level annual charges for pension cost. On the other hand, for many employers, using a long period would reduce the annual past service charge to a relatively inconsequential amount.

As explained earlier (page 43), the study prefers that pension expense be recorded in level annual amounts, varied only to give effect to changes in facts. This objective is most nearly accomplished, as to past service cost, by taking such cost into expense in substantially equal annual amounts (including interest) over a reasonable period following the inception of a pension plan. Other systematic approaches, however, are acceptable. For example, some employers may prefer to accrue past service cost in diminishing annual amounts because the number of employees to whom such cost applies diminishes as employees retire.

The fundamental concepts cited at the beginning of this chapter contribute in varying degrees to the conclusion that past service cost should be accrued over a reasonable period following the inception of a pension plan and to the selection of the accrual procedure.

The *going concern concept* supports accrual of past service cost and militates against the use of an accrual period so long that it approaches infinity (in which case only the interest on past service cost would be recognized). Assuming continuity of the employer's business, the cost of providing pensions for present employees, including past service cost, must eventually be met and so should be recognized currently.

The *matching concept* points to the use, in accruing past service cost, of the period during which the employer realizes the advantages associated with the past service element of the plan.

The *consistency concept* suggests regularity in determining the annual accrual; such regularity is an essential aspect of the conclusion stated.

## Increase in Prior Service Cost upon Amendment

When a pension plan is amended to increase retirement benefits, as often occurs, the change ordinarily applies to benefits measured by employment prior to the date of the amendment as well as to those measured by employment thereafter. The resulting increase in prior service cost is analogous to past service cost arising when a pension plan is adopted. Accounting for such an increase in prior service cost is discussed in terms of the following proposition.

PROPOSITION H. *When an amendment increases the benefits granted by a pension plan, the resulting increase in prior service cost should be charged directly to retained earnings as an adjustment of pension expense for prior years.*

ARGUMENTS IN FAVOR OF PROPOSITION H (ARGUMENTS IN FAVOR OF A CHARGE TO PRIOR YEARS)

- The increase in prior service cost applies to the years in which employees accumulated the credited service on which the increased benefits will be based.
- If the increased benefits had been in effect during the period from the inception of the plan to the date of the amendment, the applicable portion of the cost would have been provided for during that period. Hence, the entire increase in prior service cost should be charged to retained earnings as an adjustment of pension charges for prior years.

ARGUMENTS AGAINST PROPOSITION H (ARGUMENTS AGAINST A CHARGE TO PRIOR YEARS)

- The arguments against charging past service cost to retained earnings at the inception of a plan apply here with equal force. The advantages to the employer of changing the plan are for the present and the future, not for the past.
- Cost increases which result when pension benefits are raised are analogous to cost increases which result when rates of pay are raised. The former, like the latter, apply only after they have become effective.

CONCLUSION ON INCREASE IN PRIOR SERVICE COST UPON AMENDMENT

*It is a conclusion of this study that an increase in prior service cost, resulting from an amendment of a pension plan increasing benefits, should be taken into expense (together with related charges for interest) systematically over a reasonable period following the effective date of the amendment.*

The foregoing conclusion necessarily parallels the conclusion for past service cost. Again, the appropriate accrual period cannot ordinarily be identified with certainty. Again, the average remaining service lives of the employees active at the date of the amendment should be a starting point.

In practice, an increase in prior service cost resulting from an amendment liberalizing benefits is sometimes treated in the actuarial calculations as additional normal cost for current and future years, sometimes as additional past service cost. The former treatment accomplishes the objective of accruing the additional cost over a reasonable period. The latter does so if the procedure followed for past service cost conforms with the conclusions of this study and if the remaining accrual period for past service cost is an appropriate period for taking the additional prior service cost into expense. If the remaining period is unduly short, it may be desirable to spread the combined amounts over a new period.

In rare instances, modification of a pension plan may result in a decrease in prior service cost, rather than an increase. The conclusion stated is applicable in such instances, but the effect would be reversed.

## Actuarial Gains and Losses

Further questions in accounting for pension cost on the accrual basis relate to actuarial adjustments—actuarial gains and losses—which are inevitable in pension cost calculations. The method of applying such adjustments may significantly affect the amount the employer records for pension expense. The net effect of the gains and losses determined in a particular actuarial valuation is ordinarily dealt with as a single amount; if actuarial assumptions have been conservative, the net adjustment is a gain.

Two techniques for recognizing actuarial adjustments are in general use. The *immediate basis* (not ordinarily used at present for net losses) applies net gains to reduce pension expense for the year after the adjustment is determined. The *spread basis* applies a net gain or loss to current and future expense, either through the normal cost or through the past service cost.

Other approaches are, of course, possible. For example, the immediate basis may be varied so that the gains or losses, instead of being recognized in the year following determination, are recognized over a five-year period. In order to crystallize the issues, the discussion following puts aside possible variations. Viewpoints concerning the timing of recognition of actuarial gains and losses (for accounting purposes) are presented in terms of a proposition calling for use of the spread basis.

PROPOSITION I. *Actuarial gains and losses should be spread over the current year and future years.*

ARGUMENTS IN FAVOR OF PROPOSITION I (ARGUMENTS IN FAVOR OF THE SPREAD BASIS)

- If actuarial gains and losses are recognized immediately, the employer's net income for the year of recognition may be unduly increased or reduced.
- Recorded pension cost is merely an estimate of the present impact of events expected to take place in the future, actuarial gains and losses result from corrections of earlier estimates concerning such events. The corrections themselves are to some extent merely estimates, and the future may reverse them. The long-range nature of pension commitments and the extent of the uncertainties involved make it logical to take actuarial gains and losses into account by the spread method.
- To be sure, differences between accounting on the one hand and funding and tax return deductions on the other might arise if spreading actuarial gains were required. The emergence of such differences, however, is not so undesirable a consequence as to overcome the arguments in favor of spreading both gains and losses. Keeping track of such differences is a relatively simple matter.

ARGUMENTS AGAINST PROPOSITION I (ARGUMENTS IN FAVOR OF THE IMMEDIATE BASIS)

- Although actuarial gains and losses are merely estimates, they are based on the best information available and so should be recognized on the immediate basis—that is, they should be accounted for in the year when the pension accounting is based on the actuarial valuation which determines them. If actuarial gains and losses are material, consideration should be given to presenting them as adjustments of the net income of prior years.
- When the unit credit method is used, and in certain other instances, the Internal Revenue Service requires that actuarial gains be used

to reduce the maximum pension cost deduction for the year following determination. Under group annuity contracts, dividends ordinarily reduce the required contribution for the succeeding year. A requirement to spread gains for accounting purposes under such circumstances would lead to differences between book and tax accounting and would unduly complicate the necessary calculations.

CONCLUSION ON ACTUARIAL GAINS AND LOSSES

*It is a conclusion of this study that actuarial gains and losses should in most instances be spread over the current year and future years.*

In practice, many companies recognizing actuarial adjustments immediately have applied net actuarial gains in reduction of pension payments charged to expense. As a result, companies which have in most years made regular payments, and regular charges to expense, for pension cost have in some years paid and charged only a reduced amount—or, in some instances, nothing at all. This procedure clearly does not bring about an appropriate matching of revenues and expenses in the year of adjustment, since, in effect, it omits the continuing cost of providing future retirement benefits. Actuarial gains and losses are not part of the employer's operations for the year in which they are determined (or the following year). For example, the fact that the advisability of changing one or more of the actuarial assumptions became evident in a particular year does not of itself justify associating the resulting actuarial adjustment with the net income of that year. And even those gains and losses resulting from differences between actual prior experience and the assumptions used cannot logically be associated with the employer's operations for the years in which they occur.

Under another concept, actuarial adjustments would be recognized immediately, but as corrections of prior years' provisions for pension cost. This approach, seldom (if ever) used in practice, is based on the premise that if the information giving rise to the adjustment had been available in prior years, the pension expense for those years would have been correspondingly reduced (or increased). This is an unduly narrow, short-range view, whether the adjustment arises because actuarial assumptions have been changed or because experience has deviated from the assumptions used. Although actuarial techniques determine a reasonable annual charge for pension cost, they do not do so precisely. It is expected that over a long period of time the assumptions used will occasionally be changed and the actual conditions experienced will regularly deviate in some degree from the assumptions. Adjusting the employer's accounts retroactively each time this occurs would give unwarranted significance to short-range adjustments.

The objective of spreading actuarial gains and losses over the future may be accomplished in several ways: (1) The adjustment may be incorporated into future calculations of normal cost, in which case the adjustment is, in effect, amortized in decreasing annual amounts over the average remaining service lives of covered employees. Since new participants are continually being added, the period of amortization is continually being renewed. As a result, the actuarial adjustment for any year is never fully amortized, but the unamortized portion eventually approaches zero. This procedure is acceptable in most circumstances. (2) The adjustment may be applied to the unamortized prior service cost. This is acceptable unless the remaining accrual period is very short, in which case it may be preferable to use either method (1) above or method (3) following. (3) The adjustment may be treated as a separate item to be written off over a reasonable period.

*Immediate recognition preferable in some instances.* Although actuarial gains and losses should in most instances be spread into the future, circumstances may arise in which spreading is not appropriate. In general, immediate recognition may be preferable for an adjustment resulting from a single occurrence not directly related to the operation of a pension plan and not in the ordinary course of the employer's business. Thus, if as a result of the closing of a plant certain former employees are no longer covered by an employer's pension plan, an actuarial gain or loss may result, depending on the arrangements made. Although the resulting adjustment in effect represents a correction of the withdrawal (turnover) assumption, it may be distinguished because of its origin. In this example, it would be appropriate to deal with the gain or loss in the same manner as other adjustments incident to the closing of the plant.[7]

Another type of circumstance requiring special treatment of an actuarial gain or loss may arise as a result of a merger or other business combination. As a consequence of such a transaction, former employees of an acquired business may become employees of the acquiring com-

---

[7]The provisions of *Accounting Research Bulletin No. 43*, Chapter 8, "Income and Earned Surplus," 1953, may be applicable to adjustments incident to the closing of a plant.

pany and participants in its pension plan; service with the former employer may be considered in determining benefits under the new employer's plan. Such benefits may be financed by a fund established or annuities purchased by the former employer, but more frequently an unfunded prior service cost is created for the new employer at the time of the business combination. This unfunded cost is of the nature of an actuarial loss to the new employer (alternatively, a gain may result, but only in rare circumstances). The portion, if any, of such unfunded cost which would, under the criteria developed in this study, have been charged to expense in years prior to the business combination should preferably be recognized immediately by the acquiring company as follows: (a) in a purchase, as part of the cost of the assets acquired; (b) in a pooling of interests, as an adjustment of the retained earnings of the pooled company at the date of the transaction. (See, however, the discussion of retroactive adjustments beginning on page 78.)

## Unrealized Appreciation (Depreciation) of Pension Fund Investments

Important questions in accounting for actuarial gains and losses are (1) whether unrealized appreciation of pension fund investments should be recognized and (2) if so, how. In many (perhaps most) pension plan valuations, unrealized appreciation is not recognized at present. For most pension funds, long-range depreciation of investment securities has not been a problem.

Under some plans (called *equity annuity plans*), appreciation (or depreciation) of securities in a specific portfolio is assigned to participants in order to provide a measure of protection of the purchasing power of retirement benefits. The following discussion excludes such assigned appreciation (depreciation) from consideration, since it seems clear that it should not be a factor in estimating the employer's pension cost.

If the amount of the pension fund enters directly into the calculation of pension cost, as it does under some actuarial cost methods, experienced gains and losses may reduce or increase either (1) the normal cost for the present year and future years (the *spread basis*) or (2) any unfunded prior service cost (the *spread basis* if such cost is accrued). In other instances, the entire amount of any experienced gain or loss is applied to reduce or increase the employer's contribution for the year after it is determined (the *immediate basis*). With either type of actuarial cost method, it is necessary to decide whether to recognize unrealized appreciation (depreciation) of fund investments. Viewpoints are presented in relation to two propositions.

PROPOSITION J.  *Appreciation of pension fund investments should not be recognized in calculations of pension cost unless realized through sale or other disposition of the investments.*

ARGUMENTS IN FAVOR OF PROPOSITION J (ARGUMENTS AGAINST RECOGNIZING UNREALIZED APPRECIATION)

• If securities are held indefinitely in a pension fund, and only the income is used in paying pensions, appreciation or depreciation of the securities will not affect the employer's cost.

• The suggestion for valuing pension fund securities at market is inconsistent with the generally accepted accounting principle under which long-term investments are usually carried at cost in corporate balance sheets. In any event, the employer has no control over the fund itself and therefore should not recognize investment gains or losses until realized.

• Recognizing unrealized appreciation of investments could lead to unreasonable results when there are wide swings in market values, especially if the pension fund is large in relation to the unfunded cost.

• While the market value of some securities is easy to ascertain, the market value of others cannot be readily determined. Thus, recognizing changes in the market values of investments would create additional uncertainties in estimates of pension cost.

• Changes in the market values of bonds ordinarily reflect changes in the going rates of interest, rather than changes in the long-range worth of the securities. Bonds are ordinarily purchased in the expectation that they will be held to maturity. Consequently, it is inappropriate to recognize unrealized fluctuations in their market values.

• Benefits under some pension plans depend in part on compensation at or near the employee's retirement date. Under such plans, provision is ordinarily made for normal increases in compensation arising from the progression of employees through various wage rate categories. Provision is not specifically made, however, for general wage level increases, such as those which may result from inflation. Many actuaries look upon unrecognized, unrealized appreciation of pension fund assets as a hedge against the increased pension cost which may result from future wage increases arising from inflation. Therefore, unrealized appreciation should not be used in estimating pension cost.

- If appreciation is recognized, it may be necessary to change the interest assumption downward. This may have an offsetting effect so that nothing is really accomplished by using market values.

ARGUMENTS AGAINST PROPOSITION J (ARGUMENTS IN FAVOR OF RECOGNIZING UNREALIZED APPRECIATION)

- Gains on pension trust investments, when realized, provide funds for paying pensions and in the long run reduce the amount the employer must contribute. Losses have the reverse effect. It is more reasonable to believe that variations in the composition of a pension trust portfolio will eventually result in realization of changes in the values of common stock investments than to suppose the contrary. Consequently, changes in common stock values should be recognized currently in estimating pension cost.

- Recognizing changes in market values of pension trust investments is not inconsistent with present accounting principles for the long-term investments of corporations. Neither the investments of a pension fund nor the changes in their market value would be included in the employer's financial statements. Changes in investment values would be recognized only in estimating the employer's *pension expense*.

- The likelihood that market fluctuations will cause wide variations in recorded pension expense between years can be significantly reduced by choosing an appropriate procedure for recognizing appreciation. One procedure, for example, spreads each year's market variation over the current and future years, reducing or increasing the normal cost by between 5 and 8 per cent of the variation. Another procedure spreads an amount equal to a specified percentage (such as 3 per cent) of the average investment in common stocks, in lieu of the actual market variation.[8]

- The degree of uncertainty which may be introduced by recognizing appreciation of investments is not significant in relation to other uncertainties with which actuaries deal at present.

---

[8] For a discussion of procedures, see Appendix C (page 134).

- For the reasons given in an argument favoring Proposition J, changes in the market values of bonds should be recognized in estimating pension costs only if it is clear that the changes will be realized (for example, by sale of the bonds before maturity).
- Recognizing appreciation does not eliminate the hedge factor, upon which actuaries rely, against pension cost increases arising from wage increases brought about by inflation. The appreciation to be recognized is that which has already taken place. If wage levels increase in the future because of inflation, market values of common stock investments may also be expected to increase. Moreover, in most instances not all of the prior appreciation would be recognized. For example, when the market values of common stocks in a pension fund enter directly into the calculation of the normal cost, a substantial part of prior appreciation at any time remains to be absorbed as a reduction of future pension expense.
- Recognizing unrealized appreciation or depreciation of fund investments may require changing the interest assumption, but not necessarily to the extent of negating the effect of using market values. The choice of an interest assumption implies not only that the present fund balance will earn interest at the rate selected, but also that present and future contributions will earn interest at that rate.
- If unrealized appreciation is not recognized, employers in some instances may urge trustees to sell securities which have appreciated, thus creating an actuarial gain. Such a gain, if substantial, may significantly affect recorded pension expense.
- Using cost for equity securities in a pension fund produces artificial results. Different blocks of the same security, even though purchased at different prices, have no difference in value for the purpose of providing for future retirement benefits.

PROPOSITION K. *Appreciation of common stock investments in a pension fund should be recognized, but only to a limited extent.*

ARGUMENTS IN FAVOR OF PROPOSITION K (ARGUMENTS IN FAVOR OF LIMITING THE RECOGNITION OF UNREALIZED APPRECIATION)

- Appreciation of common stocks should be recognized only to the extent that the dividend rate of return is less than the yield on investments in bonds. Appreciation in excess of the yield rate on bonds represents the effect of inflation and so should not be recognized on a regular basis.

• Appreciation of common stock investments should be recognized when a plan is amended to increase benefits based on prior service, but only to the extent of the resulting increase in prior service cost.

ARGUMENTS AGAINST PROPOSITION K (ARGUMENTS AGAINST LIMITING THE RECOGNITION OF UNREALIZED APPRECIATION)

• Appreciation resulting from inflation has the same long-range effect on pension cost as appreciation resulting from other forces. Consequently, appreciation of both types should be recognized.

• Recognizing appreciation only to the extent of an increase in prior service cost resulting from a plan amendment would contradict the viewpoint adopted by this study that the cost of the increased benefits is a cost of the present and future years, rather than a cost of past periods.

CONCLUSION ON UNREALIZED APPRECIATION (DEPRECIATION) OF PENSION FUND INVESTMENTS

*It is a conclusion of this study that unrealized appreciation or depreciation of common stocks (and, in some instances, bonds and investments of other types) in a pension fund should be recognized systematically in estimating the employer's pension cost for accounting purposes.* The conclusion does not apply to amounts inuring to participants under a variable benefit pension plan.

Unquestionably, there is an element of uncertainty as to the ultimate realization of appreciation or depreciation of common stocks. It seems more reasonable to believe, however, that variations in the composition of a pension trust portfolio will eventually result in realization of changes in common stock values (thus translating the value changes into increases or decreases in long-range pension cost) than to suppose the contrary. In the case of bonds and investments of other types, analysis will disclose whether it is more reasonable to believe that changes in value will ultimately be realized or to believe that they will not.

Several techniques are available for recognizing unrealized appreciation or depreciation of investments of a pension fund. This study favors the use of a procedure which does not give undue weight to short-term market fluctuations.[9]

## Employee Service Before Coverage

Under some pension plans, employees are eligible for coverage when they are hired if they are within the classification of employees entitled to participate (for example, members of a certain bargaining unit); under other plans, there are additional requirements as to age or length of service or both. Some plans, on the other hand, state the conditions an employee must meet in order to be eligible to receive retirement benefits but otherwise do not deal with coverage.

One of the purposes of age and service requirements is to exclude the youngest employees and those with the least tenure, the ones most likely to leave the employer within a relatively short time. Excluding these employees simplifies actuarial calculations by reducing the number of people who must be considered and makes it possible to predict more accurately the turnover that will be experienced among employees who are considered.

Although excluding employees not covered is clearly appropriate in determining amounts to be paid, a question arises as to whether excluding them is also appropriate in determining accounting charges. Discussion of this question is presented in relation to the following proposition.

PROPOSITION L.   *Expense under a pension plan should not be accrued in respect of service by employees who may become eligible for coverage but who have not met eligibility requirements as to age, length of service, or both.*

ARGUMENTS IN FAVOR OF PROPOSITION L (ARGUMENTS IN FAVOR OF INCLUDING ONLY COVERED EMPLOYEES)

• To contend that pension cost should be accrued for an employee before he is covered by a pension plan is similar to contending that past service cost should be charged to periods prior to the inception of the plan. No pension cost is incurred for an employee prior to the time he is covered; this is true even in those instances wherein qualifying service is recognized in determining the amount of benefits. The fact that pension benefits are in part measured by service in a particular

---

[9] For a discussion of procedures, see Appendix C (page 134).

year or years does not of itself justify identifying the cost so measured as an expense of that period.
- The increase in employment cost resulting when an employee becomes covered by a pension plan is real. It is comparable with the increases in cost which result when employees receive periodic increases in pay.
- Including employees in pension calculations before the employees attain covered status would make the calculations more burdensome without improving the usefulness of the resulting estimates of pension cost. In many instances, additional calculations would be required because those made for funding purposes would continue to include only covered employees.
- If employees are included in the calculations without regard to eligibility requirements, it will usually be necessary to increase the assumed rate of turnover. Ordinarily, an increase in pension expense resulting from the former change will be substantially offset by a decrease resulting from the latter.

ARGUMENTS AGAINST PROPOSITION L (ARGUMENTS IN FAVOR OF INCLUDING EMPLOYEES NOT YET COVERED)

- The cost of providing pensions applies to the entire working lives (after the inception of a plan) of the employees whom the plan will benefit—not just the portion of their working lives during which they are covered by the plan.
- Unless pension cost is accrued while an employee is accumulating qualifying service, an abrupt increase in recorded employment cost occurs when the employee becomes a participant and, hence, a factor in the actuarial calculations.
- The procedure suggested is inadequate in the case of a plan which defines eligibility for receipt of benefits but not for coverage. For example, if an employee may retire under such a plan at age sixty-five with twenty years of service, it may be argued that he does not become eligible for coverage until age forty-five. Excluding employees from pension cost calculations until they reach age forty-five, however, would not produce a satisfactory accounting result.

CONCLUSION ON EMPLOYEE SERVICE BEFORE COVERAGE

*It is a conclusion of this study that present employees who may reasonably be expected to become participants in a pension plan should be included in calculations of the cost of the plan for accounting purposes.*

In practice, it may be desirable to exclude employees during an initial period of service in which turnover is high (for example, three years). This may simplify the calculations without significantly changing the annual amount.

## Interest on Differences Between Pension Cost Accruals and Contributions

The actuarial cost methods used in assigning the cost of a pension plan to periods of time, whether for accounting or for funding purposes, assume that contributions by the employer (and in some instances by employees) will provide part of the money needed to pay benefits and that earnings on pension fund investments (called *interest* for simplicity) will provide the balance. If the employer's contributions exceed those assumed, the portion of the total cost which will be met by interest increases, and the employer's future contributions are correspondingly reduced. If, on the other hand, the employer's contributions are less than those assumed, the interest which would otherwise have been earned on fund investments must eventually be contributed by the employer if the expectations of the procedure adopted for accounting purposes are to be fulfilled.

*It is a conclusion of this study that, if the contributions to a pension fund differ from the accounting charges, the latter should include (or be reduced by) interest on the difference between the actual pension fund and a theoretical fund which would have been produced on the basis of the accounting charges.* The method of calculation is illustrated by the following examples.

*Example 1*

An employer's annual contributions to a pension fund, determined under the *entry age normal method* using an interest rate of 3 per cent, comprise: (1) the normal cost and (2) $67,216 for amortization, based on a twenty-year period, of past service cost of $1,000,000. In accounting for pension cost, the employer charges the normal cost to expense each year and accrues the past service cost over a thirty-year period. Under these circumstances, the annual charge to pension expense for past service cost would be $51,019 (the annual factor necessary to accrue $1,000,000 over a thirty-year period with interest at 3 per cent), less amounts equivalent to interest (at 3 per cent) on the excess of the payments over the accrual charges. The following table illustrates the accounting entries and balances which would result (disregarding the normal cost).

## CHAPTER 3: TIMING THE CHARGES TO EXPENSE

| Year | Amount charged to pension expense — Thirty-year accrual factor | Reduction for interest° | Amount charged | Amount paid (twenty-year amortization) | Deferred charge carried in the balance sheet (end of year) |
|---|---|---|---|---|---|
| 1  | $51,019 | $  —   | $51,019 | $67,216 | $16,197 |
| 2  | 51,019  | 486    | 50,533  | 67,216  | 32,880  |
| 3  | 51,019  | 986    | 50,033  | 67,216  | 50,063  |
| 10 | 51,019  | 4,936  | 46,083  | 67,216  | 185,680 |
| 20 | 51,019  | 12,204 | 38,815  | 67,216  | 435,216 |
| 21 | 51,019  | 13,056 | 37,963  | —       | 397,253 |
| 22 | 51,019  | 11,918 | 39,101  | —       | 358,152 |
| 25 | 51,019  | 8,302  | 42,717  | —       | 233,678 |
| 30 | 51,019  | 1,457  | 49,562  | —       | —       |

° On the excess of payments over accruals.

*Example 2*

The facts in the second example are the same as those in the first, except that the past service cost is to be paid over forty years instead of twenty years. In this instance, the annual charge to pension expense for past service cost would be $51,019 (the annual factor necessary to accrue $1,000,000 over a thirty-year period with interest at 3 per cent) plus amounts equivalent to interest (at 3 per cent) on the excess of the accrual charges over the payments. The following table illustrates the accounting entries and balances which would result (disregarding the normal cost).

| Year | Amount charged to pension expense — Thirty-year accrual factor | Addition for interest° | Amount charged | Amount paid (forty-year amortization) | Credit carried in the balance sheet (end of year) |
|---|---|---|---|---|---|
| 1  | $51,019 | $  —   | $51,019 | $43,262 | $ 7,757 |
| 2  | 51,019  | 233    | 51,252  | 43,262  | 15,747  |
| 3  | 51,019  | 472    | 51,491  | 43,262  | 23,976  |
| 10 | 51,019  | 2,364  | 53,383  | 43,262  | 88,927  |
| 20 | 51,019  | 5,845  | 56,864  | 43,262  | 208,434 |
| 30 | 51,019  | 10,524 | 61,543  | 43,262  | 369,050 |
| 31 | —       | 11,073 | 11,073  | 43,262  | 336,861 |
| 32 | —       | 10,107 | 10,107  | 43,262  | 303,706 |
| 35 | —       | 7,032  | 7,032   | 43,262  | 198,150 |
| 40 | —       | 1,261  | 1,261   | 43,262  | —       |

° On the excess of accruals over payments.

*Example 3*

The facts in the third example are the same as those in the second, except that in some years the employer's payments for past service cost vary from those which would have been made under the schedule initially established. The following table illustrates the effect of varying payments during the tenth through the twentieth years (disregarding the normal cost).

| Year | Thirty-year accrual factor | Addition for interest°° | Amount charged | Amount paid | Credit carried in the balance sheet (end of year) |
|---|---|---|---|---|---|
| 10° | $51,019 | $2,364 | $53,383 | $ 43,262 | $ 88,927 |
| 11 | 51,019 | 2,668 | 53,687 | 140,000 | 2,614 |
| 12 | 51,019 | 78 | 51,097 | — | 53,711 |
| 13 | 51,019 | 1,611 | 52,630 | — | 106,341 |
| 14 | 51,019 | 3,190 | 54,209 | — | 160,550 |
| 15 | 51,019 | 4,816 | 55,835 | — | 216,385 |
| 16 | 51,019 | 6,492 | 57,511 | 130,092 | 143,804 |
| 17 | 51,019 | 4,314 | 55,333 | — | 199,137 |
| 18 | 51,019 | 5,974 | 56,993 | — | 256,130 |
| 19 | 51,019 | 7,684 | 58,703 | 120,000 | 194,833 |
| 20° | 51,019 | 5,844 | 56,863 | 43,262 | 208,434 |

*Amount charged to pension expense*

° The amounts for years prior to year ten and subsequent to year twenty are the same as in Example 2.
°° On the excess of accruals over payments.

*Example 4*

The facts in the fourth example are the same as those in the second, except that instead of amortizing the past service cost the employer merely pays interest on it. The results in this instance are similar to those in Example 2. After the accrual period, however, the annual charge to expense for past service cost, representing interest, is equal to the amount paid. The following table illustrates the accounting entries and balances which would result (disregarding the normal cost).

| Year | Thirty-year accrual factor | Addition for interest° | Amount charged | Amount paid (interest) | Credit carried in the balance sheet (end of year) |
|---|---|---|---|---|---|
| 1 | $51,019 | $ — | $51,019 | $30,000 | $ 21,019 |
| 2 | 51,019 | 630 | 51,649 | 30,000 | 42,668 |
| 3 | 51,019 | 1,280 | 52,299 | 30,000 | 64,967 |
| 10 | 51,019 | 6,406 | 57,425 | 30,000 | 240,961 |
| 20 | 51,019 | 15,838 | 66,857 | 30,000 | 564,791 |
| 30 | 51,019 | 28,514 | 79,533 | 30,000 | 1,000,000 |
| Thereafter | — | 30,000 | 30,000 | 30,000 | 1,000,000 |

*Amount charged to pension expense*

° On the excess of accruals over payments.

As the examples show, the adjustment for interest may increase annually in some periods and decline annually in others. While this variation may at first appear undesirable, the theory underlying it is sound. An employer making pension fund contributions which are less than the amounts of pension expense accrued on the books may be expected to earn a return on the additional assets thus retained for use in operations. This return offsets (but probably does not match exactly) the additional pension expense resulting from the interest adjustment. Conversely, an employer making contributions greater than the expense accrued may be expected to suffer a reduction in earnings. This reduction offsets (but probably does not match exactly) the reduction in pension expense resulting from the interest adjustment.

## TYPES OF PLANS NOT PREVIOUSLY DISCUSSED

Earlier, to simplify the discussion, consideration of certain types of plans was deferred.

### Certain Insured Plans

Among the plans remaining to be discussed are insured plans in which the funding instrument consists of individual insurance or annuity policies or a group annuity contract or contracts. Under such plans, the employer may have less latitude in determining the annual contribution than is typical under trusteed plans and plans funded through deposit administration contracts or similar arrangements.

If individual policies are used, premiums are ordinarily determined under the *individual level premium method*, following the insurance company's rate structure. Under a group annuity contract, the employer's payments for normal cost are ordinarily determined by the *unit credit method*, and past service cost is ordinarily amortized, but the payments may vary in amount.

The criteria stated earlier for determining accounting charges under trust fund plans apply equally to the insured plans described. Payments to insurance companies under such plans ordinarily meet the criteria proposed in this study for determining charges to expense on the accrual basis, with three exceptions: (1) the study accepts the actuarial cost methods ordinarily used in the insured plans but prefers the entry age normal method; (2) under group annuity plans, the amounts of the payments for past service cost may be determined arbitrarily, whereas the study concludes that past service cost should be recognized systematically; (3) under the insured plans, the immediate basis is ordinarily used in recognizing actuarial gains (for example, dividends, and credits due to employee turnover), whereas the study concludes that significant actuarial adjustments should ordinarily be spread over the current year and future years.

## Defined-contribution Plans

Defined-contribution plans, also set aside earlier, are of two types. Under one type, known as a *money-purchase plan*, the employer's contributions are determined for, and allocated with respect to, specific individuals, usually as a percentage of compensation. The benefits for each employee are the amounts which can be provided by the sums contributed for him. Under this type of plan, the employer's contributions *for* a given period (not necessarily those made *in* the period) are the proper amounts to be charged to expense.

The other, more common, type bears the name *defined-contribution plan*. It states the pension benefits or the method of determining them, as does a defined-benefit plan. A *defined-contribution plan*, however, is ordinarily drawn up to accompany a separate agreement that provides a formula for calculating the employer's contributions (for example, a fixed amount for each ton produced or for each hour worked, or a fixed percentage of compensation). Initially, the benefits stated in the plan are those which the contributions expected to be made by the employer can provide. In relating benefits and contributions, one of the actuarial cost methods described in Chapter 2 (page 26) is used. The calculation may be made (1) on the basis that the defined contributions are to include amortization of past service cost over a selected period (such as 30 years) or (2) on the basis that the defined contributions are to include only interest on the past service cost. Ordinarily, if the defined contributions include an allowance for amortization of past service cost, it would be unlikely for indications to exist at the inception of a *defined-contribution plan* necessitating an accrual pattern differing from the payment pattern.

If the defined contributions subsequently appear to be inadequate or excessive for the purpose of *funding* the stated benefits on the basis originally contemplated (for example, because of a change in the level of the employer's operations), either the contributions or the benefits (or both) may be adjusted in subsequent negotiations. Under such circumstances, or if the defined contributions differ from an accounting charge conforming with the criteria set out in this study, determining an appropriate accounting accrual will require careful analysis based on the facts of each situation.

## Unfunded Plans

The conclusions stated earlier for funded plans apply equally to unfunded plans. Ordinarily, however, the annual charges to expense under an unfunded plan would exceed the annual charges under an otherwise identical funded plan because under the former there would be no fund to provide earnings to meet part of the cost. Under an unfunded plan, the pension expense element for interest on the excess of accruals over funding (page 68) would be at a maximum. This would be true even for employers which segregate assets in their balance sheets, calling the amount a "pension fund." Since the earnings on such a fund are transactions of the employer, they should be included in the employer's income rather than offset against pension expense.

# OTHER CONSIDERATIONS

## Responsibility for Calculations of Pension Cost

The calculations required in assigning the cost of a pension plan to periods of time involve complicated actuarial considerations. Consequently, actuaries play a leading role. Nevertheless, the corporate executive responsible for the employer's financial statements ordinarily bears the responsibility for the amount of pension cost recorded. In exercising this responsibility, the executive may discuss with the actuary the choice of actuarial cost method and actuarial assumptions. After the calculations have been made, the executive may review them. In both instances, his objective would be to satisfy himself that the actuarial cost method used is acceptable for accounting purposes, that the actuarial assumptions, *taken together,* are reasonable, and that both the actuarial cost method and the assumptions have been applied in a manner acceptable for accounting purposes.[10]

Actuarial cost methods and the factors to be considered in applying them have been discussed earlier in this chapter. In considering actuarial assumptions, it is important not to judge specific ones entirely apart from the others. For example, the actuarial assumption as to the earnings of a pension fund (called *interest* for convenience) often attracts attention. The interest assumption should not be appraised alone, however, because the estimates of pension cost, rather than the individual assumptions, are the central issue. As a further example, it is important in considering the interest rate to consider also the treatment of unrealized appreciation (or depreciation) of pension fund investments. Recognizing unrealized appreciation (or depreciation) may require a change in the interest assumption; conversely, present and future appreciation (or depreciation) may be recognized indirectly by the choice of assumed interest rate.

## Income Tax Allocation

In the past, the amounts which employers have deducted for pension expense in their Federal income tax returns have in most instances equalled the accounting charges because both have been based on the

---

[10] The responsibility of independent public accountants for pension cost in financial statements they examine is an *auditing* matter and, hence, is not considered in detail in this study on *accounting* for the cost of pension plans. Some commentators have implied that it is inappropriate for independent public accountants to inquire into the factors underlying an actuary's recommendation as to the amount to be charged to expense for pension cost. These commentators may not be fully aware that independent public accountants, in discharging their overall responsibility for reporting on financial statements, must frequently evaluate conclusions of experts on whose judgment a client's management has relied. It is usual, for example, to discuss with engineers their estimates of the cost of completing complicated contracts, to inquire of lawyers as to the possible outcome of important legal matters and to ascertain the basis on which tax counsel (if employed) has estimated tax liability. An independent public accountant has the same degree of responsibility for pension cost that he has for other financial statement elements of comparable materiality and may appropriately discuss the pension calculations with the actuary. In general, his objective would be the same as that of the financial executive responsible for the financial statements. In pursuit of this objective, he might examine the actuary's calculations to the extent necessary to confirm his understanding of the procedure followed.

amounts paid.[11] If the conclusions of this study are adopted, tax return deductions for pension expense may more frequently differ from accounting charges because the former presumably will continue to equal payments, while the latter may not.

When such differences occur, taxable income for the current year is greater or less than if the accounting method followed in the financial statements had been followed in the tax return as well. Ordinarily there is a reasonable expectation that taxable income for subsequent years will be correspondingly less or greater. Under present practice, such circumstances usually result in income tax allocation.[12]

## Materiality

The relative significance of the matters considered in this study may be expected to vary from employer to employer and from year to year for a particular employer. The study intends, however, to deal only with situations wherein the matters at issue are important. Materiality, while not specifically mentioned, is an implicit factor in each phase of the study; none of the conclusions reached is intended to apply when the amounts involved are so small that in fact it does not matter how they are handled.

## Comparability of Financial Statements

A general objective of the research program of which this study is part is to narrow areas of difference and inconsistency in accounting practice. In the minds of many, this objective means enhancing the degree to which the financial statements of different companies are comparable by eliminating accounting differences (whether in principles, practices or methods) not justified by differences in circumstances. If comparability, in this sense, were to be acknowledged as an objective, the conclusions of the study would require reappraisal.

As an example, the study concludes that several actuarial cost

---

[11] The Federal income tax consequences of pension plans are discussed in Chapter 2 and in Appendix A.

[12] Accounting for income taxes is discussed in: *Accounting Research Bulletin No. 43*, Chapter 10B, "Income Taxes," 1953; and *Accounting Research Bulletin No. 44 (Revised)*, "Declining-balance Depreciation," 1958. A study on accounting for income taxes is being conducted under the research program of which this study is part.

methods may appropriately be used in determining pension expense. To achieve comparability, however, it would be necessary either to select a single method or to specify the circumstances under which each acceptable method should be used. If a single method were to be selected, this study would choose the *entry age normal method,* for the reasons indicated earlier. Specifying the circumstances under which the other methods should be used might prove difficult. One or another might be chosen, for instance, if an increasing or declining trend in annual pension cost were considered an appropriate goal, or if it were believed that the amount of the annual charge for the cost of a pension plan should depend on whether insurance policies are used in funding the plan. From the viewpoint of this study, however, such criteria do not seem appropriate.

It should be obvious that universal adoption of the *entry age normal method* (or any other actuarial cost method) would not equalize pension charges among companies, nor would the comparability objective intend or desire this result. Pension cost would vary among companies because pension benefits vary, because the age distribution of employee groups varies, and because judgments vary in selecting actuarial assumptions. Companies would also have different funding policies, and while funding would not influence the accounting charges directly, it would influence them indirectly by affecting both the interest on unfunded cost and the portion of cost ultimately met by fund earnings. Thus, variations in pension charges would remain, but the variations would result from differences in facts or in judgment—not from differences in the methods of calculation.

As another example, this study concludes that past service cost should be accrued over a reasonable period of time following the inception of a plan. In applying the comparability objective, it would be necessary to identify the accrual period more precisely, perhaps by selecting a specific period such as the average remaining service life of employees initially covered.

## Pension Cost Incurred Outside the United States

For the most part, this study has analyzed issues in terms of pension practices in the United States. Many U. S. companies, however, incur pension expense in other countries, either through divisions or through subsidiaries. Although there are variations, practices in other countries concerning private pension plans are generally comparable with U. S.

practices. The conclusions reached in this study are intended to apply to pension cost incurred in other countries as well as in the United States.

## TRANSITION TO RECOMMENDED PROCEDURES

Some employers at present account for the cost of pension plans in conformity with the conclusions of this study. Others will change their procedures in varying degrees if they adopt the study's conclusions. The principal changes which may be necessary are discussed below.

## Principal Changes

### Consistency in recording pension expense

At present, some companies vary the amount of their annual pension payment (and hence the annual charge to expense) on the basis of factors such as the amount of cash available or the level of earnings before deducting pension cost. Under present procedures, employers may omit pension expense in some years. Under the procedures proposed, however, there would be an annual charge for pension expense.

### Actuarial cost methods

Some employers determine pension expense on the *pay-as-you-go* basis or by *terminal funding*. This study, however, regards both procedures as unacceptable for use in accrual accounting. In addition, many employers at present use actuarial methods which this study regards as acceptable, but not preferable. Employers adopting the *entry age normal method,* viewed as preferable, might experience substantial changes in annual pension expense.

### Accruing past service cost

Some companies do not amortize (or accrue) past service cost, but fund (and charge to expense) only an amount representing interest on this cost element. Others pay irregular amounts. The payments, however determined, are ordinarily charged to expense. This study, however, recommends that past service cost be taken into expense systematically over a reasonable period following the inception of a pension plan.

*Increase in prior service cost upon amendment*

Many companies account for an increase in prior service cost, resulting from an amendment of a pension plan increasing benefits, as if it were an element of the initial past service cost, which they do not amortize. This study, however, recommends that such an increase in prior service cost be taken into expense systematically over a reasonable period following the effective date of an amendment.

*Recognizing actuarial gains and losses*

Companies which at present recognize significant actuarial gains and losses immediately would spread them over the current and future years in conforming their accounting with the conclusions of this study.

*Appreciation (depreciation) of pension fund investments*

At present, relatively few companies recognize changes in the market value of pension fund investments in determining pension expense. This study, however, recommends that such changes be taken into account for common stocks and in some instances for bonds and other investments.

## Putting the Changes into Effect

The problem of how to put into effect any necessary changes in procedures remains to be discussed. The following solutions should be considered:

**1.** As of the date of change, determine the cumulative difference between the provisions for pension expense previously made under procedures not meeting the criteria developed in this study and provisions which would have been made in conformity with the study's criteria. The amount may be either a charge (if prior provisions have been inadequate) or a credit (if prior provisions have been excessive). Account for this amount (giving appropriate consideration to the effect of income tax) as an adjustment of results of operations for prior years (for purposes of this discussion, it will be assumed that such an adjustment would be carried directly to retained earnings)[13] or as an adjustment of other prior transactions. As an illustration of an adjustment of the latter type, if employees have become participants in the

---

[13] Adjustments of prior years' operating results are discussed in *Accounting Research Bulletin No. 43*, Chapter 8, "Income and Earned Surplus," 1953.

plan as a result of a merger or other business combination, it may be appropriate to apply part of the "cumulative difference" as a correction of the entries made to record the business combination (see the discussion on page 60). In years following the date of change, charge operations with pension expense determined in conformity with the criteria developed in this study.

**2.** As of the date of change, determine the "cumulative difference" described in Solution 1. In subsequent years, charge operations with an amount consisting of (a) pension expense determined in conformity with the criteria developed in this study and (b) an allocated portion of such "cumulative difference." Because the latter factor would in effect be a correction of results of operations for years prior to the date of change, the criteria developed in this study would have no significance in selecting the number of future years to which this element would be allocated.

**3.** As of the date of change, determine the amount of prior service cost not previously funded or otherwise accounted for (in most instances, this amount will be the unfunded prior service cost). In subsequent years, charge operations with an amount consisting of (a) normal cost determined in conformity with criteria developed in this study and (b) an allocated portion of prior service cost not previously accounted for. The latter factor would be determined substantially as if the plan had been adopted or amended as of the date of change. It would include (as an unidentified increase or reduction) a portion of the "cumulative difference" described in Solution 1.

For some companies, the "cumulative difference" described in Solution 1 would be relatively minor. For example, unrealized appreciation of common stocks in a pension fund which should have been recognized in the past (under the criteria developed in this study) may be approximately offset by past service cost which should have been charged to expense (under such criteria). If the "cumulative difference" were immaterial, the results under all of the procedures described above would be substantially the same. This study, however, must consider the merits of each procedure for general application when the effect of variations would be material.

*Theoretical considerations*

In theory, acceptance of the criteria for determining pension cost developed in this study would require that the criteria be applied retroactively (Solution 1). If they were not, pension expense which logically applies to prior years would be charged against the operations of future years. Thus, the study's conclusions, although accepted nominally, would not be applied in fact.

From the contrary point of view, some may support spreading the adjustment on the basis that such a procedure would be similar to the spreading procedures recommended by this study for factors such as past service cost and actuarial gains and losses. This analogy, however, is unsound. The cost factors that this study has recommended for spreading are elements of a continuing flow of pension cost to be determined under a set of criteria consistently applied. On the other hand, if an adjustment such as that now under discussion arises, it will have resulted from a radical change in the accounting principles (or methods of applying them) applicable in determining pension expense.

It may also be argued, in support of spreading the adjustment, that if revised procedures are applied retroactively substantial amounts of pension cost may not be charged to expense for any year, being charged instead to retained earnings. On the other hand, this undesirable result would be overcome, at least in part, in any future reports of results of operations for prior years. That is, the applicable portion of any retroactive adjustment would be taken into consideration in restating prior year figures.

On balance, theoretical considerations point to a conclusion favoring retroactive adjustment (Solution 1). There are, however, important practical objections to retroactive adjustment.

*Practical considerations*

For one matter, a *requirement* for retroactive adjustment would be a departure from precedent. Retroactive application of statements on accounting principles issued by agencies of the American Institute of Certified Public Accountants has not been mandatory in the past.[14]

Another important practical consideration relates to companies whose rates for charging customers are regulated by government agencies. For such companies, Solution 1 (retroactive adjustment) might create a *practical* problem paralleling one of the *theoretical* arguments against retroactive adjustment—that substantial amounts of pension cost might bypass the income statement. For companies in nonregu-

---

[14] A provision of *Accounting Research Bulletin No. 47* permits charges to retained earnings for pension cost in certain circumstances by companies adopting the preferred procedure expressed in the Bulletin. Only a few companies have made such charges.

lated industries, this would improve future earnings in comparison with earnings determined under either Solution 2 or Solution 3. For regulated companies, however, a similar comparative increase in future earnings would be unlikely because regulated rates are ordinarily set at a level intended to permit recovery of operating costs and expenses and to provide a return on invested capital. On this basis, pension cost charged to retained earnings in Solution 1 would not be recognized in rate determinations. Under Solution 2, the portion of pension expense calculated separately as a correction of charges for prior years (element b) might likewise not be recognized. It can be argued, of course, that regulatory authorities ought to permit companies subject to their jurisdiction to use either Solution 1 or Solution 2 in their published financial statements but to spread the adjustment into the future (Solution 2 or Solution 3) in reports prepared for purposes of rate determination. Not all (perhaps not any) of such authorities would do so, however; as a result, regulated companies using either Solution 1 or Solution 2 might suffer serious financial losses. Employers having cost reimbursement contracts, either with government agencies or with private companies, might be similarly penalized.

Still another practical problem arises from difficulties that would be encountered in determining the "cumulative difference" to be charged or credited to retained earnings in Solution 1 or spread over future years in Solution 2. Ordinarily, the "cumulative difference" would be that portion of prior service cost not previously funded or otherwise accounted for which would have been charged to expense in prior years under the criteria developed in this study. In some instances the determination would be relatively simple, but the presence of a number of variables would complicate most calculations.

To illustrate, the entire unfunded prior service cost of a plan which has been in effect without change for, say, twenty years (an unusual situation) might be charged to retained earnings under Solution 1. The calculations would become more complicated, however, if (for example):

- The employer wished to adopt a period longer than twenty years for accruing past service cost.
- The plan had been amended to increase benefits, thus creating additional elements of prior service cost.
- After the inception of the plan, the employer had acquired one or more other companies, bringing new employees having prior service credits into the plan.

- Actuarial gains, which under this study's criteria are recognized on the spread basis, had been recognized on the immediate basis.

The difficulties in calculation would be severe in many instances. Frequently, it would be necessary to make arbitrary assumptions as to the composition of prior service cost not previously accounted for. It would also be necessary to assume that the employer's pension *funding* (in some cases, the complete absence of funding) would not have been different had the employer used different pension accounting procedures.

*Summation on transition*

Thus, none of the solutions proposed above (page 78) is satisfactory on both theoretical and practical grounds. Further, resolution of the issue must be predicated upon resolution of a broader question—the general question of retroactive application of changes in accounting principles—which is beyond the purview of an inquiry into methods of accounting for the cost of pension plans. Consequently, this study does not propose a conclusion as to the procedure which should be adopted in putting into effect the criteria developed in the study for assigning pension cost to periods of time. However, except that precedent for *requiring* retroactive adjustments is lacking and except in special circumstances such as those of companies in regulated industries and companies having cost reimbursement contracts, the study views retroactive adjustment (Solution 1, page 78) as preferable.

# 4

# Presentation in Financial Statements

This chapter is concerned with the presentation of information about pension plans and pension cost in the financial statements of the employer. Chapter 2 briefly described present disclosure practices. Before discussing the nature and extent of the information which *should be* presented, we will consider the existing guidelines.

### EXISTING GUIDELINES

*ARB 47*,[1] discussed in Chapter 2, deals with disclosure in paragraphs 7 and 8:

> 7. ... Accordingly, for the present, the committee believes that, as a minimum, the accounts and financial statements should reflect accruals which equal the present worth, actuarially calculated, of pension commitments to employees to the extent that pension rights have vested in the employees, reduced, in the case of the balance sheet, by any accumulated trusteed funds or annuity contracts purchased.
>
> 8. The committee believes that the costs of many pension plans are so material that the fact of adoption of a plan or an important amendment to it constitutes significant information in

---

[1] *Accounting Research Bulletin No. 47*, "Accounting for Costs of Pension Plans," 1956. *ARB 47* is reproduced in Appendix E.

financial statements. When a plan involving material costs is adopted, there should be a footnote to the financial statements for the year in which this occurs, stating the important features of the plan, the proposed method of funding or paying, the estimated annual charge to operations, and the basis on which such annual charge is determined. When an existing plan is amended to a material extent, there should be similar disclosure of the pertinent features of the amendment. When there is a change in the accounting procedure which materially affects the results of operations, there should be appropriate indication thereof. If there are costs of material amount based on past or current services for which reasonable provision has not been, or is not being, made in the accounts, appropriate disclosure should be made in a footnote to the financial statements as long as this situation exists.

Disclosure requirements applicable to financial statements filed with the Securities and Exchange Commission are set forth in Rule 3-19 of the Commission's Regulation S-X:

> General Notes to Balance Sheets . . . (e) Pension and retirement plans—(1) A brief description of the essential provisions of any employee pension or retirement plan shall be given. (2) The estimated annual cost of the plan shall be stated. (3) If a plan has not been funded or otherwise provided for, the estimated amount that would be necessary to fund or otherwise provide for the past service cost of the plan shall be disclosed.

## DISCLOSURE IN THE BODY OF THE FINANCIAL STATEMENTS

Questions of presentation may be discussed in relation to (1) information which should appear in the body of the financial statements and (2) information which should appear in notes. The discussion immediately following concerns the first category. Some information, of course, may appropriately be presented in either category.

### Balance Sheet

*Unfunded prior service cost*

It is sometimes suggested that the amount of unfunded prior service cost (in particular, the amount of unfunded past service cost) of a

## CHAPTER 4: PRESENTATION IN FINANCIAL STATEMENTS

pension plan represents a liability which should be shown in the employer's balance sheet. Those who would so present past service cost at the inception of a plan might also present a deferred charge of equal amount, the latter to be amortized by charges to expense in succeeding years.

The notion that past service cost is a liability may arise for a number of reasons. One is the fact that this cost element is measured by service in the past. The terminology of pensions reinforces the liability concept. Juxtaposing "past service" and "cost" seems to imply a liability. Moreover, actuaries sometimes use "accrued" and "liability" in referring to past service cost, in the expressions "accrued actuarial liability" and "supplemental liability," although in so doing they do not intend to imply the existence of a liability in the accounting sense. Beyond this, the practice of including in pension payments an amount representing *interest* on unfunded past service cost suggests that this cost is a liability.

In Chapter 3, however, this study concluded that prior service cost in general and past service cost in particular, although measured by employee service in years prior to creation of the cost, should be included in expense of subsequent years. Prior (past) service cost has no accounting significance until it is recognized as an expense under an appropriate procedure (see Chapter 3). Consequently, such cost should appear in the employer's balance sheet only to the extent that accounting charges determined in accordance with the criteria developed in this study differ from payments.

In Chapter 3 (page 34), the possibility was discussed that, if accounting charges for pension cost exceed payments, employees may contend (for example, in the event of termination of a pension plan) that the resulting balance sheet credit is payable to them (or to a pension trust). Consequently, it may be desirable to avoid using words such as *accrued* and *liability* in describing pension cost in an employer's balance sheet. Instead, a descriptive expression such as *Provisions for pension cost in excess of payments* or *Pension cost charged to expense but not funded* may be preferable.

### Vested rights

In some instances, especially in the early years of a plan, the present value of pension rights which have vested in employees may exceed the amount in the pension fund. It is sometimes suggested that the unfunded amount ought to appear as a liability in the employer's balance sheet.[2] This study concludes that the appropriate treatment depends on the terms of the specific plan. If employees have legally enforceable claims against the employer for vested pension rights (a relatively rare circumstance), any excess of the actuarial present value of such rights over the amount of the pension fund (or annuity contracts purchased) should be shown as a liability. If the cost of the plan is being accounted for in conformity with the recommendations of this study, the additional amount recorded as a liability should not be charged to expense but should be carried forward as a deferred charge to the operations of future years.

## Statement of Income

### Charge for pension expense

The amount of pension expense must be disclosed in financial statements filed with the Securities and Exchange Commission. Many employers also disclose pension expense in financial statements issued to stockholders although the information is not called for by *ARB 47*. The SEC requirement and the disclosure practice in reports to stockholders have developed, at least in part, because of the existing variations in accounting practices. If the range of variations is narrowed as proposed in this study, there will be less reason for employers following the recommended procedures to disclose the amount of pension expense. There would, for example, be no more reason to disclose the amount than to disclose the amount of direct labor or the amount of vacation pay.

### Interest

The employer's contributions to a pension fund provide part of the money which will be needed to pay benefits. Earnings on the funds contributed (called *interest* for simplicity) provide the balance. Thus, the contributions are, in effect, reduced by fund earnings. On the other hand, employers' contributions customarily include an element representing interest on the unfunded balance of prior service cost. Under present practice, employers charge their pension contributions entirely to pension expense. For the sake of completeness, this study should consider whether an employer ought to record interest income or expense in connection with a pension plan.

---

[2] See, for example, paragraph 7 of *Accounting Research Bulletin No. 47*.

# CHAPTER 4: PRESENTATION IN FINANCIAL STATEMENTS

An employer has no interest income or expense in connection with a pension plan funded through a trust or an insurance company; the earnings on the funds contributed are not income of the employer but of the trust or the insurance company. Similarly, the amounts included in employers' contributions as interest on unfunded prior service cost are not interest expense but rather are part of the total amount of pension cost. The foregoing holds true for the interest element of accrual charges whether or not funded.

On the other hand, an employer may have interest income in connection with an unfunded plan if funds are set aside for purposes of the plan. Since the earnings on such segregated funds arise from transactions of the employer, they should not be offset against pension expense but should be included in income.

## DISCLOSURE IN A NOTE

Opinions vary widely as to the nature and extent of information concerning pension plans which may be useful to readers of financial statements. At present, in addition to the amount of pension cost in expense (discussed earlier), information which may appear in notes to financial statements includes the amount of unfunded prior service cost, the basis for funding (accruing) such cost, and a brief explanation when a pension plan is adopted or amended. Additional information which might be considered for disclosure includes the following:

> The amount of funds in the hands of a trustee or insurance carrier, the amounts of securities held (by major categories), and the method of valuing investments.
>
> The date of the most recent actuarial valuation and the name and affiliation of the actuary.
>
> The actuarially determined present value of vested pension rights.
>
> The major provisions of the pension plan (to be disclosed annually).
>
> The actuarial factors and methods used to determine the charge to operations and the payments to the fund.
>
> Changes in (a) the actuarial factors or methods used to compute the charge to operations or the payments to the fund or (b) the accrual period for unfunded prior service cost, and the effects on (i) the financial statements, (ii) the liability for income tax and (iii) the payments to the fund.

In accrual accounting, the amount corresponding to the unfunded prior service cost (which includes unfunded past service cost) is the amount remaining to be charged to operations. The idea that this amount should be disclosed in a note, either as a cost incurred in the past or as a commitment, is no more valid than the idea, discussed earlier (page 84), that the amount should appear as a liability in the balance sheet. Consequently, routine disclosure of the amount of prior service cost remaining to be charged to operations is unnecessary.

Routine disclosure of other information is justified only if the information is useful and is required for a fair presentation of financial position and results of operations.[3] In this context, it should no more be necessary to disclose the terms of a pension plan in financial statements, even in the year adopted or substantially modified, than to disclose a wage increase or a liberalization of the formula for determining employees' vacations. Beyond this, much of the information which might be disclosed would be of no value to a reader of financial statements unless he had at his command a wide range of other information about employment cost, including such matters as wage rates, productivity levels and working rules. If the recommendations of this study are adopted, the existing range of variations in accounting practices will be significantly limited. Therefore, disclosure may properly be diminished rather than expanded.

Although routine disclosure of information about pension plans and pension cost seems unnecessary, disclosure of a significant change in the procedures for determining pension expense seems essential. Such a change may involve management's selection of a different accounting practice or may be made because of altered conditions. Examples are: a change in the basis of accounting (e.g., from the pay-as-you-go basis to the accrual basis); a change in actuarial cost method (e.g., from the unit credit method to the entry age normal method); a change in an actuarial assumption (e.g., from an interest assumption of 3.5 per cent to an assumption of 4 per cent); a change in the period

---

[3] The Federal Welfare and Pension Plans Disclosure Act requires the administrator of a pension plan to file reports with the Secretary of Labor. The reports include certain items of information sometimes suggested for disclosure in financial statements, and the availability of the reports in the files of the Department of Labor is sometimes cited as a reason for not disclosing the information in financial statements. This study, however, does not view the availability of information in another source as relevant to the question of whether financial position and results of operations are fairly presented by financial statements which do not disclose the information.

for accruing past service cost (e.g., from twenty-five years to twenty years); a change in the level of pension expense arising because past service cost has been fully accounted for (e.g., in the year following the final year of a twenty-five year accrual period). If such a change materially affects the comparability of the financial statements as between accounting periods, the change and its effect should be disclosed in a note.[4]

## CONCLUSIONS

### Amounts Appearing in the Balance Sheet

*It is a conclusion of this study that the unfunded prior service cost of a pension plan is not a liability which must be shown in the balance sheet of an employer. Ordinarily, the amount to be shown for pension cost in the employer's balance sheet is the difference between the amount which has been charged to expense in accordance with the recommendations of this study and the amount which has been paid. If, as may occur in rare instances, participants' vested rights are a liability of the employer, the unfunded present value should appear as a liability; if the employer accounts for the cost of the plan in conformity with the recommendations of this study, the amount should be carried forward as a deferred charge to operations.*

### Disclosure

*It is a conclusion of this study that routine pension disclosures should not ordinarily be necessary in the financial statements of companies whose accounting for pension cost conforms with the recommendations of the study. If, however, a change in an accounting practice or an accounting change necessitated by altered conditions affects the comparability of the employer's financial statements as between accounting periods, the change and its effect should be disclosed.*

---

[4] *Statements on Auditing Procedure No. 33*, Chapter 8, "Consistency of Application of Generally Accepted Accounting Principles," 1963.

## Comments of B. Russell Thomas

Briefly, my position concerning accrual of pension costs is as follows:

1. Annual normal cost and interest on past service cost is the true long-range measure of annual costs of a pension plan. If costs are to be determined on a "going concern" basis without regard to either (a) the possibility of termination of the plan or (b) any legal obligation assumed by the employer to contribute a greater amount, normal cost and interest would constitute the appropriate accounting charge.

2. Contributions to a pension fund in excess of normal cost and interest, whether made voluntarily by the employer or made because of the employer's legal liability under the plan, should be treated as added costs for the year in which made, unless it can be shown that they are abnormal contributions which should be spread over a limited period of years. (For example, payment of all or a substantial portion of the past service cost in a single year should result in charges spread over a period of several years.)

## Comments of W. A. Walker

Past service costs are generally related to past service so there is no logic in saying that past service costs must be written off in a specific pattern in order to match costs and revenues when in reality there is no relation between such costs and current revenues. Thus, if the unfunded past service cost is amortized over a specified period of years, the pension cost shown in the earlier years of the plan would not be relevant to the benefit values being earned in those years. Furthermore, the contribution level will change sharply at the end of the period. If, however, the accrual for pension cost is limited to the normal cost plus interest on past service cost, the accounting accruals would not only furnish the greatest stability of pension cost from year to year but would more closely approximate the objectives of matching current cost and current revenues.

Such past service costs are undertaken for the benefit of the plan as a whole, and not necessarily for the benefit of any individual employee, and as such the benefits to be expected from them are indefinite in duration. As a practical matter, charges in respect of past service may be viewed as being largely in the nature of a strengthening of the plan, and as such should be governed by funding policies determined by management, and with adequate disclosure. Consequently, a change in the period over which past service costs are provided, or the failure to make any provision in a given period, should not result in qualification with respect to fairness of presentation nor consistency of application of accounting principles; however, if the amount of the change is material, there should be disclosure of this fact in the notes to the financial statements. I believe the above recommendations are more compatible with the "going concern" concept which is one of the underlying principles upon which the research study recommendations were made.

It is indeed inconsistent to contend that there is no requirement to show any part of the past service cost on the balance sheet when it is created, but that a fixed portion of it becomes a liability—if not funded—each year for some set number of future years.

Showing a balance sheet liability for past service costs could have adverse effects. First, it could result in penalizing companies which adopt actuarial methods that result in greater funding. Thus, a company using a level percentage cost method and not making past service payments might have considerably more assets in its pension fund than competitors which make past service payments but determine current service costs by using another accepted method. Such company would, nevertheless, be required to reflect a pension accrual on its books despite the fact that its ratio of fund assets to total pension liabilities was considerably in excess of the ratio of the other companies. A company, if confronted with this situation, might tend to adopt actuarial assumptions for accounting purposes that would minimize the recorded liability or the amount funded. Second, if a company actually recorded such a liability, it could lead to pressure to fully fund an amount which may require borrowing merely to place it in a fund to the detriment of stockholders and employees.

APPENDIX A[1]

# The Pension Background

The private pension movement in the United States is rooted in one of the most significant economic, social, and political developments of the twentieth century—the progressive increase in the number and proportion of the population in the aged category (age sixty-five and over). Some conception of the magnitude of the problem can be grasped from the following brief account of the demographic, social, and economic influences at work.

## ECONOMIC BASIS OF THE OLD-AGE PROBLEM

### Population Trends

During the last half century, the growth in the number and proportion of the aged population in the United States has been phenomenal. Only 4.3 per cent of the population in 1910 was sixty-five and over, whereas in 1960, 9.2 per cent fell in that category. This spectacular increase reflects the combined influence of a decline in the birth rate, an increase in life expectancy, and the curtailment of

---

[1] This appendix is a condensation of Chapter 1, "Underlying Forces," of *Fundamentals of Private Pensions,* Second Edition, by Dan M. McGill, published in 1964 for the Pension Research Council. In the interest of brevity, footnotes which appeared in the original work, including those disclosing sources of statistics and quotations, have been omitted. Readers interested in this and other additional information are referred to Professor McGill's book.

immigration. The long-run decrease in the birth rate was reversed during World War II and the birth rate has since remained at a relatively high level, but population experts are reluctant to predict precisely the future course of fertility. The tremendous extension in life expectancy recorded during the last fifty years as a result of advances in medical science and a rise in general living standards will certainly not be duplicated during the next half-century, but as medical science devotes more and more study to the diseases of old age, further gains can be anticipated. Immigration, which once contributed large numbers of young people to the United States population, has been a negligible factor for the last several decades and is not expected to assume a more important role.

## Employment Opportunities for the Aged

The increase in the proportion of old people has been accompanied by a decline in the employment opportunities of the aged, chiefly among males. In 1890, 68.3 per cent of aged males were in the labor force, but by 1960 the percentage had shrunk to 30.4 per cent. Many factors have contributed to the decline, but one of the most significant has been the transition to an industrial and predominantly urban economy. Whereas persons in agricultural employment can continue working, at least part time to advanced ages, industrial employees, because of the physical demands of their jobs or employer personnel policy, must retire at a relatively early age. In recent years the hard core of long-duration unemployment at the younger ages and the generalized effect of automation have placed increasing stress on early retirement. Other factors which have influenced the trend include the improvement in longevity, extension of social insurance and pension programs, and the widespread acceptance of age sixty-five as the normal retirement age.

## Capacity to Save for Old Age

The implications of the foregoing are broadened by the lessened capacity of individuals to save for their own old-age maintenance. Relentless pressure on all classes of individuals to spend all or the greater portion of their income has made systematic provision for old age a secondary consideration for the majority of families; the enormous fiscal needs of the Federal Government have led to the imposition of personal tax rates which render it difficult for even those persons in the higher income brackets to make adequate provision for their old-age needs; inflation has impaired the ability of fixed-income persons to save and has undermined the purchasing power of funds already accumulated by any group; finally, the depression of the 1930's swept away savings.

## Changed Concept of Filial Responsibility

In earlier days it was not a matter of particular concern if persons reached old age without adequate means of support. Elderly members of a family resided with and were supported by younger members. Increasing urbanization of society and other economic and social developments have weakened the traditional approach to old-age care and support. As a result society is looking increasingly to government and employers for old-age support.

# PUBLIC PENSION PROGRAM

The limitations of the individual approach to old-age financial security have led to the establishment of governmental programs. The most comprehensive and significant is the Federal Old-Age, Survivors, and Disability Insurance System (social security). This program has a profound impact on private pension plans.

## Federal Old-Age, Survivors, and Disability Insurance

*Coverage*

Federal Old-Age, Survivors, and Disability Insurance (hereafter designated OASDI) is the national program of old-age social insurance created by the Social Security Act of 1935 and, as such, is the foundation of all other programs of old-age income maintenance. The broad objective is to cover all gainfully employed persons, including the self-employed. With minor exceptions, coverage for eligible persons is compulsory and immediate. Today nine out of every ten gainfully employed persons are covered under the system. The principal exclusions are railroad workers (who have their own plan which is partially coordinated with OASDI), Federal employees under any Federal retirement system, employees (who have not elected to be covered) of state and local governments, self-employed physicians, irregularly employed farm and domestic workers, and very-low income self-employed persons.

*Benefits*

*Eligibility for retirement benefits.* Benefits under the OASDI program are paid as a matter of statutory entitlement and are not generally conditioned on a showing of need. Retirement benefits are payable upon actual retirement at or after age sixty-two (benefits are permanently reduced for retirement before age sixty-five) and the satisfaction of a service requirement. In effect, the benefits vest after ten years of service (a shorter period for men over age twenty-five and women over age twenty-two on January 1, 1959), with their amount being subject to diminution through periods of noncoverage or lower earnings. Benefits are conditioned on actual retirement, the test of which has been substantial withdrawal from covered employment. Thus, the law provides for reduction of $1.00 in benefits for each $2.00 of annual earnings in excess of $1,200 and not in excess of $1,700 and of $1.00 in benefits for each $1.00 of annual earnings in excess of $1,700. In no case, however, are benefits withheld for any month in which the beneficiary's remuneration as an employee is $100 or less, and in which he renders no substantial services in self-employment.

*Nature and level of benefits.* The OASDI program provides retirement, disability, and survivorship benefits, all of which are based on the insured's "primary insurance amount." The present benefit formula produces a primary insurance benefit for the retired individual approximately equivalent to 30 per cent of the first $4,800 of covered annual earnings, with the combined benefit to the individual and his aged wife being about 45 per cent of the covered annual earnings. The disability benefit payable to an individual without dependents is about 30 per cent of the first $4,800 of covered annual earnings, while the family benefits for a disabled person may amount to 60 per cent of his covered earnings. Finally, the survivorship benefits payable to a widow and children run to the order of 50 to 60 per cent of the covered annual earnings.

*Financing*

The cost of the OASDI program, including both benefit and administrative expenditures, has been borne by the covered employees and their employers. The funds have been derived from a payroll tax levied in equal proportions on employers and employees and since 1951 from a tax on covered earnings of the self-employed. The rate of contribution in 1963 is 3-⅝ per cent each for wage earners and their employers (5-⅖ per cent for self-employed persons, who pay approximately one and one-half times the employee rate). The ultimate rate, scheduled for 1968 and thereafter, is 4-⅝ per cent each.

The present system of financing is neither pay-as-you-go nor full reserve. Contributions have been more than adequate to meet benefit and administrative expenditures but much less than adequate to accumulate a full reserve. It has been estimated that, without future income from contributions, the existing fund of $21 billion would not be capable of meeting the obligations of the program to those persons who have already begun to draw benefits, not to mention the accrued liabilities for those persons who are still working. Indeed, as of the end of 1962, the present value of the benefits to be paid to those persons already on the benefit rolls was estimated to be $117 billion and the total net accrued liability of the system, including that for all persons who have contributed to the program (representing the excess of estimated future benefit outgo over future contributions for these persons) was estimated at $312 billion as of January 1, 1962.

## Federal Staff Retirement Plans

Entirely distinct from the national old-age insurance program, several staff retirement plans have been established under the aegis of the Federal Government. Designed with one notable exception, to provide old-age benefits to various categories of Federal employees, these plans bear a close resemblance to private pension plans. Largest of the Federal plans and, in fact, the largest single employer pension plan in existence, is the Civil Service Retirement System. Other retirement plans for Federal civilian employees cover members of the foreign service, employees of the Federal Reserve Banks, employees of the Tennessee Valley Authority, and members of the Federal judiciary. On the periphery of Federal staff plans is the Railroad Retirement System. This program is unique in the American pension field in that it is operated for a group of private employers but is underwritten by the Federal Government and the benefits are administered by the Federal Government.

## State and Local Retirement Systems

A heterogeneous assortment of public pension plans has been established at the state and local level. These plans differ widely in their details, but in most jurisdictions separate plans exist for policemen, firemen, and teachers, all other employees, if covered at all, being lumped together into a general retirement system.

## Other Public Pension Programs

Public pension programs financed entirely from general revenues represent another broad source of old-age benefits and deserve brief mention. The best known of these programs is Old-Age Assistance, intended to provide benefits to those indigent old persons who could not qualify for OASDI benefits. This objective was to be accomplished through a system of Federal grants-in-aid to states. The Federal Government is currently bearing about five-eighths of benefit expenditures and slightly more than one-half of the costs of administration. The public pension program provided through the Veterans Administration is another important source of old-age income.

# THE PRIVATE PENSION MOVEMENT

## Rationale

Industrial pensions appeared on the American scene during the last quarter of the nineteenth century, but only within the last twenty-five years have they assumed any significance in the old-age financial picture. In the beginning, private pension benefits were universally regarded as gratuities from a grateful employer in recognition of long and faithful service. The payments were usually discretionary, the employer assuming no legal obligation to provide benefits. In fact, most plans stated in specific terms that no employee rights were being created thereunder and reserved to the employer the right to deny benefits to any employee and to reduce or terminate benefits which had already commenced. A few plans promised to continue benefit payments to retired employees but made no commitment to active employees. These plans exemplified the gratuity theory of pensions.

As the years went by, certain groups, anxious to encourage and strengthen the pension movement, sought to place on the employer a moral obligation to provide pensions to superannuated employees. As early as 1912, one student of the old-age problem wrote: "From the standpoint of the whole system of social economy, no employer has a right to engage men in any occupation that exhausts the individual's industrial life in ten, twenty, or forty years, and then leave the remnant floating on society at large as a derelict at sea." This point of view was frequently expressed during the next few decades, being the subject of widespread debate in the early 1920's. It was adopted by the United Mine Workers and used by that organization in its 1946 campaign to establish a welfare fund. The concept received its most influential endorsement in the report of the fact-finding board in the 1949 steel industry labor dispute. The board wrote, in part, as follows:

"As hereinafter amplified, we think that all industry, in the absence of adequate government programs, owes an obligation to workers to provide for maintenance of the human body in the form of medical and similar benefits and full depreciation in the form of old-age retirement—in the same way as it does now for plant and machinery."

The human depreciation concept has been supplanted—or supplemented—in some quarters, by the theory that pensions are nothing more than deferred wages. The latter concept holds that an employee group has the prerogative of choosing between an immediate wage increase and a pension plan, and, having chosen the latter, is entitled to regard the benefits as deferred wages.

With the tendency for the parties to a collective bargaining agreement to express the employer's pension commitment in terms of wage equivalency, such as "x" cents per hour, and given the safeguards surrounding a formal, Treasury-approved pension plan, these conditions would seem to be fulfilled when the benefits are collectively bargained. In the absence of collective bargaining, the relationship between pension contributions and foregone immediate wages would, at best, be only approximate. Nevertheless, "deferred wages" is gaining increasing acceptance as a label for the collective benefits associated with a pension plan.

The tenuous relationship between wages foregone and pension benefits received in the case of individual participants—occasioned by the absence or deferment of vesting—has caused some to look for another explanation of pensions. One view is that an old-age retirement benefit represents a differential wage payment in recognition of the special contributions, not reflected in wage payments, of a long-service employee to the firm. These contributions include the preservation of the folklore of the industry, fostering of loyalty to the firm and its traditions, and the transmission of technical skills from older to younger generations of workers.

Still another view of pensions is that they are a device, instituted and nourished by business firms, to meet the social problem of old-age economic dependency. Persons holding this view see a duty on the part of the business community in a private enterprise society to provide the mechanism through which gainfully employed individuals, by direct contributions or foregone wages, can make provision for their own old-age needs. This obligation can be discharged only through the establishment and operation of plans which measure up to minimum standards of benefit adequacy, benefit security, and financial solvency. Advocates of this view assert that only if the business community meets this challenge can social insurance schemes be confined to their proper bounds.

Persuasive as some of these theories are, it is doubtful that the private pension movement can be explained in terms of any one social or economic philosophy. Its rationale lies in broad and conflicting forces that do not lend themselves to definitive characterization. One might conclude that the only tenable explanation of the development is business expediency. Yet this expression is so pervasive that it furnishes only the vaguest of clues as to the specific forces that motivate employers to adopt pension plans. It might be helpful, therefore, to examine some of the significant factors and developments that have made it seem expedient to an employer to establish a pension plan.

## Forces Influencing the Growth of Private Pension Plans

*Productivity of the employee group*

Unquestionably, one of the most compelling employer motives in adopting a pension plan is the desire to increase the productivity of his employees. This motive is usually mixed with others, including a sincere desire to provide financial security to retired or superannuated employees. Nevertheless, unless the employer believes that the cost of the pension plan can be substantially offset by savings in other phases of company operations, including production costs, he may not be overly receptive to the idea of pensions.

On balance there is little doubt that the efficiency of the labor force is enhanced through the establishment of a pension plan. American industrial development has reached the stage where most concerns of any size now, or soon will, face the problem of dealing with large numbers of employees near or beyond normal retirement age. The first possible approach to this problem is to discharge employees without retirement benefits as they become superannuated. A second possibility is to retain superannuated employees on the payroll at full or reduced pay but in a capacity commensurate with their diminished ability and vitality. The third approach, and in the great majority of cases the only one offering a satisfactory solution, is for the employer to establish a formal pension plan. This permits the employer to remove over-age employees from the payroll in an orderly fashion, without fear of adverse employee and public reaction, and to replace them with younger, presumably more efficient, workers.

The installation of a pension plan is thought to boost production in other ways. It is argued, for example, that the morale of the employee group will be elevated. While a pension plan is definitely a positive morale factor, one may wonder whether its influence among rank-and-file employees, particularly those distant from retirement, is not overshadowed by more immediate considerations, such as wages, hospitalization benefits, and working conditions.

It is also argued that the establishment of a pension plan will reduce turnover and hence the cost of training replacements. This argument is difficult to evaluate, since it is impossible to isolate the influence of a pension plan. It is of some relevance that the highest rate of turnover occurs among employees who because of their youth or short service may not be eligible for membership in the plan or, even if active participants, may be only slightly influenced by the promise of a retirement benefit. Moreover, any reduction in turnover will be reflected in higher pension costs, since a higher percentage of employees will qualify for benefits.

A pension plan is a particularly effective instrument of personnel policy with respect to supervisors, who tend to be more responsive to the stimulus of a pension plan and to carry out their responsibilities more effectively. Furthermore, it is especially important that a means exist whereby the executives and other supervisors can be readily retired at an appropriate time after they have passed the peak of effectiveness. Related to this is the importance of keeping open the channels of promotion. Finally, a pension plan unquestionably enables an employer to attract and hold better-qualified executives than would otherwise be possible.

*Tax inducements*

Related to the foregoing in the sense that both are cost-reducing factors are the tax inducements offered by the Federal Government. The Revenue Act of 1942 is frequently cited as the genesis of the favorable tax treatment of private pension plans, but the real beginning of such policy is found in much earlier legislation. Before the enactment of any legislation directed specifically at private pensions, reasonable payments made as pensions to retired employees or as contributions to a trust to fund current pension credits were deductible from the employer's gross income, but only as an ordinary and necessary business expense and then only if, together with other payments, they represented reasonable compensation. Payments to a trust to fund past service credits or to place the trust on a sound financial basis were not deductible, and the income of the trust was currently taxable to the employer, employees, or the trust, depending on the provisions of the trust instrument.

Beginning with the Revenue Act of 1921, the statutes have progressed toward the law under which pension plans operate today. At the present time, most pension plans are "qualified"—that is, they meet certain requirements of Section 401(a) of the Internal Revenue Code of 1954 and of Sec. 1.401 of the Income Tax Regulations. These requirements are as follows:

1. There must be a trust, contract, or other legally binding arrangement. The plan must be in writing and must be communicated to the employees. Furthermore, it must be a permanent and continuing program.

2. The plan must be for the exclusive benefit of the employees or their beneficiaries, and it must be impossible prior to the satisfaction of all liabilities under the plan for any part of the corpus or income to be diverted to any other use. In fact, the trust agreement or other applicable document must contain a specific statement to the effect that no funds can be diverted.

3. The plan must benefit employees in general and not just a limited number of favored employees. To meet this requirement the plan must cover either a prescribed percentage of employees or a classification of employees found by the Commissioner of Internal Revenue not to be discriminatory in favor of officers, shareholders, supervisors, or highly compensated employees.

4. The plan must not discriminate in favor of officers, shareholders, or highly compensated employees with respect to contributions or benefits. Variations in contributions or benefits are permissible so long as the plan in its overall operations does not discriminate in favor of that class of employees with respect to which discrimination is prohibited. It is of special significance that contributions or benefits based on remuneration excluded from the OASDI wage base may differ from contributions or benefits within such base as long as the resulting differences in benefits are approximately offset percentage-wise by the benefits available under the Federal OASDI program. If such an equivalence obtains, the plan is said to be integrated with OASDI.

5. A plan to provide retirement benefits to employees or their beneficiaries will be deemed a pension plan if either the benefits payable to the employee or the contributions required of the employer can be determined actuarially. Benefits are not definitely determinable if

funds arising from forfeitures on termination of service, or for other reasons, may be used to provide increased benefits for the remaining participants rather than being used to reduce employer contributions. There is an implication that the plan should be actuarially sound, but Treasury approval of a plan carries with it no certification that contributions under the plan will be adequate to provide the benefits.

The principal tax advantages that flow from qualification of a pension plan under applicable tax law are: (1) employer contributions to the plan are deductible, within specified limits, as ordinary and necessary business expenses for Federal income tax purposes; (2) employer contributions to the plan are not includable in the taxable income of the participating employees until made available to them; and (3) the investment earnings on funds accumulated under the plan are not subject to income taxation until disbursed in the form of benefits. Of lesser importance to the employer firm and rank-and-file employees, but attractive to more highly compensated participants, are additional advantages associated with the treatment of employer contributions under certain specifically defined circumstances. These advantages are: (4) if, upon a participant's death or other separation from service, the entire amount standing to his credit is distributed within one taxable year of the distributee, a long-term capital gain results for purposes of Federal income taxation; (5) upon the death of a participant, any payments to beneficiaries other than the deceased's estate attributable to employer contributions are excludable from the decedent's gross estate for Federal estate tax purposes; and (6) the exercise or non-exercise by a participant of an election or option whereby an annuity or other payment will become payable to any beneficiary at or after the participant's death is not considered a transfer for Federal gift tax purposes to the extent that the value of the refund feature is attributable to employer contributions.

*Pressure from organized labor*

A third broad factor influencing the adoption of pension plans has been the attitude of organized labor. Until the late 1940's or early 1950's organized labor was, in the main, either indifferent to the pension movement or openly antagonistic to it. Over the years, however, attitudes changed to such an extent that in 1949, when another round of wage increases seemed difficult to justify, a large segment of organized labor demanded pensions in lieu of wages. The way was paved for such a switch when a Federal court ruled that pensions are a bargainable issue.

This arose out of a union grievance filed with the National Labor

Relations Board in 1946, alleging that the unilateral action of the Inland Steel Company in enforcing a policy of compulsory retirement at age sixty-five constituted a breach of a provision of the general labor contract relating to separation from service. The Inland Steel Decision (by the Court of Appeals for the Seventh Circuit) established a legal framework within which no employer during the term of an applicable labor agreement can install, alter, or terminate a pension plan for organized workers without the assent of the labor bargaining unit. This obligation rests on the employer whether or not the plan was installed prior to certification of the bargaining unit and whether or not the plan be compulsory or voluntary, contributory or noncontributory.

Since 1949, organized labor has been a vigorous and potent force in the expansion of the private pension movement.

*Social pressure*

A final factor that has encouraged the spread of pension plans is the social and political atmosphere that has prevailed during the last quarter century. During that period the American people have become security conscious. The economic upheaval of the early 1930's swept away the life savings of millions and engendered a feeling of insecurity that shook the very foundations of the country. Prominent among the proposals for economic reform were those that envisioned social action in the area of old-age income maintenance. The Federal OASDI program was the outgrowth of these proposals.

Since the Federal program was deliberately designed to provide only a "floor of protection," the way was left clear for supplemental benefits to be provided through private measures. In view of the general inability—or unwillingness, as some would have it—of the individual to accumulate through his own efforts the additional resources required, society has come to expect the employer to bear a share of the burden. The employer may successfully shift his share of the costs to the consumer, but a great deal of social pressure is exerted on the employer to provide the mechanism through which additional funds can be accumulated. If the employer chooses not to install a formal pension plan, he may find that social pressure forces him to take care of his superannuated employees in some other manner. In anticipation of such a development, employers are turning in increasing numbers to formal pension programs as the most economical and satisfactory method of meeting the problem.

APPENDIX B

# Public Policy and Private Pension Programs

The Committee on Corporate Pension Funds and Other Private Retirement and Welfare Programs was constituted by the President of the United States to conduct a study which would include "a review of the implications of the growing retirement and welfare funds for the financial structure of the economy, as well as a review of the role and character of the private pension and other retirement systems in the economic security system of the nation, and consideration of how they may contribute more effectively to efficient manpower utilization and mobility." The January 1965 report of the Committee to the President[1] contains the following summary.

## SUMMARY OF MAJOR CONCLUSIONS AND RECOMMENDATIONS

### Development of Private Retirement Plans

*Conclusions:*

Private retirement plans now cover about twenty-five million workers, about half of the employees in private nonfarm establish-

---

[1] President's Committee on Corporate Pension Funds and Other Private Retirement and Welfare Programs, *Public Policy and Private Pension Programs*, Jan. 1965, pp. vi-xvi.

ments. They pay almost $2¾ billion a year in benefits to nearly two and one-half million beneficiaries. Their status as a major financial institution is reflected in their accumulated reserves of over $75 billion, in their annual accumulations of $6½ billion, and in their annual benefit payments of almost $2¾ billion a year.

It is estimated that by 1980 the number of employees covered by retirement plans will increase to forty-two million, or three out of five employees then expected to be in private nonfarm establishments. The number of beneficiaries will increase to about six and one-half million in 1980. According to these projections, plans will continue to build substantial reserves since the contributions paid into the funds, together with the funds' earnings, will be far in excess of benefit payments. Under the assumed conditions, total contributions, which amounted to nearly $7 billion in 1964, are expected to rise to about $11 billion a year by 1980, while benefit payments during the same period will increase to around $9 billion annually. Total reserves will grow to about $225 billion by 1980.

## The Public Interest in Private Retirement Plans

*Conclusions:*

Although the development of private retirement plans has largely been the result of business and labor initiative, public policy has encouraged and protected these plans through tax laws, labor relations statutes, standards of fiducial obligations of trustees, and more recently through specifically designed legislation requiring public disclosure of various aspects of retirement and welfare plans.

The prevailing tax provisions for private pensions make it possible to provide private pensions at a substantially lower cost than that which would result if no special tax provisions were available for pensions. Regardless of how the worker and the employer may share the benefits—in the form of higher pensions or reduced costs—which the special tax provisions for pensions make possible, it is evident that the advantages for both employers and workers are very significant. The loss of revenue to the Federal Government as a result of this special tax treatment is estimated to be more than $1 billion annually.

Several points underline the breadth and depth of the public interest in private retirement plans:

(1) They represent a major element in the economic security of millions of American workers and their families.

(2) They are a significant, growing source of economic and financial power.

(3) They have an important impact on manpower in our economy.

(4) They have a major, growing significance for Federal taxpayers because the special tax concessions reduce the tax base and put more burden on other tax sources.

## Relation of Private Plans to the Public Retirement Program

*Conclusions:*

The public program will continue to be the Nation's basic instrument for assuring reasonably adequate retirement income to workers, their widows and dependents.

Private pension plans should continue as a major element in the Nation's total retirement security program. Their strength rests on the supplementation they can provide to the basic public system.

The basic justification for the indirect public subsidy involved in favored tax treatment lies in the social purposes served by private pension plans. In view of these social purposes, public policy should continue to provide appropriate incentives to private plan growth, and by improving the basic soundness and equitable character of such plans, set a firmer foundation for their future development. Because protection will always be far from complete, private pension plans cannot be a substitute for public programs, but public policy can encourage developments which will provide supplementary retirement benefits to a growing proportion of the Nation's workers and will provide greater assurance that the promised benefits will be paid.

Continuing attention will be necessary to assure that the combined benefits available through OASDI and supplementary private pensions, for those receiving them, are reasonably related to wage levels and living standards in the economy.

## Private Pensions, Labor Mobility, and Manpower Policy

*Conclusions:*

Private pensions, along with seniority and other benefits based on length of service, tend to reduce labor mobility by tying workers to a particular employer. While the effect of private pensions on mobility is significant, it is limited and selective. However, there is cause for concern in the selective impediments to mobility now erected by private pension plans and in the possibility that such plans in the future will not permit a rate of mobility among mature workers sufficient to accommodate a rapid rate of technological change.

Employers should be encouraged to adopt more widely those types of pension plans which do not involve significantly higher costs for older workers, in preference to those types which involve greater differences in cost between new employees in different age groups. However, legislation affecting private pensions is not recommended as a means of minimizing the use of rigid age limits in hiring.

The government should not attempt to regulate compulsory retirement practices, which should be left to private decision. However, employers should be encouraged to adopt flexibly administered systems of retirement. Measures to compel earlier retirement are not desirable or suitable as a general means of dealing with unemployment problems.

## Vesting

*Conclusions:*

The advantages which vesting brings to the private pension system are the following:

(1) As a matter of equity and fair treatment, an employee covered by a pension plan is entitled, after a reasonable period of service, to protection of his future retirement benefit against any termination of his employment.

(2) Vesting also provides special advantages to the employer.

(3) By making private pension benefits more widely available, vesting strengthens the Nation's program for retirement protection.

(4) Vesting enhances the mobility of the work force.

The values of vesting extend beyond the interests of the participants in pension plans. Benefits to the entire economy are involved, including the strengthening of economic security for retired workers and the effective operation of the Nation's system of labor markets.

*Recommendations:*

A vesting requirement is necessary if private pension plans are to serve the broad social purpose justifying their favored status. The Internal Revenue Code should be amended to require that a private pension plan, in order to qualify for favored tax treatment, must provide some reasonable measure of vesting for the protection of employees. Several suggestions are made regarding the most effective method for implementing this requirement without creating obstacles to the future growth of the private pension system. The Committee suggests a system of graded deferred vesting based solely on service applicable to both single and multiemployer plans. An appropriate transition period should be provided, and special procedures made available to plans whose costs would be increased by more than 10 per cent as a result of this recommendation, the recommendation on funding, or a combination of the two.

## Funding for Financial Solvency

*Conclusion:*

Pension plans without adequate funding may turn out to be empty or only partially fulfilled promises. The minimum standards for funding under present tax law do not assure adequate funding. The setting of standards for adequate funding, therefore, becomes an important public concern.

*Recommendations:*

The present minimum standard for funding needs to be strengthened by changes along the following lines:

(1) As a minimum standard of funding for *stated benefit* plans, the plan should be required to fund fully all current service liabilities and to amortize fully all accrued liabilities over a period that roughly approximates the average work life of employees but not more than 30 years.

(2) As a minimum standard for funding of *fixed contribution* plans, the contribution commitments of the plan should be realistically related to benefits promised and actually paid.

(3) The funding process of every qualified plan should be certified at the inception of the plan and periodically thereafter by an actuary with acceptable professional qualifications.

(4) The funding process should be subject to review by the Internal Revenue Service on the basis of guidelines or ranges of standards with respect to such actuarial assumptions. The guides should be specified by the Internal Revenue Service with the advice and consultation of a public advisory body of actuaries and other interested parties.

(5) Concurrent with actuarial certification, a determination should be made by a professionally qualified public accountant with respect to the value of pension fund assets.

(6) An appropriate transition period should be provided, and special procedures made available to plans whose costs would be increased by more than 10 per cent as a result of this recommendation, the recommendation on vesting, or a combination of the two.

## Portability and Insurance

*Conclusions:*

Two proposals are worthy of serious study to help fulfill the long-range promise of the private pension system:

(1) The possibility of some institutional arrangement for transferring and accumulating private pension credits.

(2) A system of insurance which, in the event of certain types of termination, would assure plan participants credit for accrued benefits.

## Inequities Under the Tax Laws

*Conclusion:*

Present laws permit many serious inequities in qualified private retirement plans and in the tax treatment of benefits distributed by such plans.

*Recommendations:*

(1) The option which qualified retirement plans now have to cover only salaried or clerical employees should be eliminated, unless there is a showing of special circumstances.

(2) The maximum period for which coverage of any employee can be deferred by a qualified plan should be reduced from five to three years.

(3) Employees of tax-exempt institutions should be given tax favored treatment for pension benefits earned after the date of the change only where they participate in tax qualified plans.

(4) An appropriate dollar limitation on contributions to qualified corporate pension plans for any employee or a commensurate limitation on benefits should be required, as to benefits earned after the date of the change, in order to prevent abuse and restrict favored tax treatment to private plans which furnish benefits consistent with the public interest.

(5) Qualified plans should be permitted to continue to integrate with OASDI, but, as to benefits earned after the date of the change, the employer should be given credit for no more than one-half of the social security benefit.

(6) The present provision treating lump-sum distributions of retirement benefits as long-term capital gains should be replaced, as to benefits earned after the date of the change, by an appropriate averag-

ing device which might take into account the individual's future income status.

(7) The special tax treatment of distributions of employer securities to employees should be eliminated, with respect to appreciation in value arising after the date of the change.

(8) Gift and estate taxes should apply to transfers of interests in qualified retirement plans in the same manner as they apply to transfers of similar types of property.

(9) Deferred profit-sharing plans should be required to provide for employers' contributions in accordance with a predetermined formula.

(10) The Committee's vesting requirement should also apply to deferred profit-sharing plans designed primarily to provide retirement benefits but in such cases reallocation of forfeitures among the remaining participants would be prohibited. In the case of all other deferred profit-sharing plans, a provision granting immediate vested rights to all covered employees should be required.

(11) An appropriate transition period should be provided and special procedures established for those plans whose costs would be substantially increased by these recommendations.

## Financial Aspects of Retirement Plans

*Conclusions:*

The total amount of investments held by private retirement funds has increased from $12 billion at the end of 1950 to over $75 billion at the end of 1964. A further increase to around $225 billion is projected by 1980. However, the Committee does not believe there are sufficient grounds for recommending regulation of the size of retirement funds or of their rate of capital accumulation.

By 1964, the noninsured funds were investing half of their new resources in common stocks. This shift has certainly been one of the factors contributing to increases in common stock prices, particularly for the higher grade stocks, although it would be very difficult to estimate the quantitative importance of this single factor.

In view of the wide legitimate differences regarding the most advantageous balance of retirement funds investments, the Committee does not believe it would be desirable on the basis of evidence to date to require conformity to a prescribed rule with respect to the proportion of stocks to other investments.

## Protecting the Interests of Employees in the Investments of Retirement Funds

*Conclusions:*

Whatever the type of investments made by retirement funds, such investments should be made honestly, conscientiously and prudently; it is important that there be the greatest practicable degree of assurance on these points.

This Committee recognizes the need for additional measures for the protection of the interests of employees, but doubts whether a major problem is the lack of appropriate standards of prudence. On the basis of present evidence, the Committee does not propose the substitution of a new set of statutory standards for the recognized standards of fiducial responsibility, although there appears to be a need for strengthening statutory provisions for assuring compliance with these standards.

Full disclosure of relevant facts is a prerequisite for self-help and for the enforcement of statutory measures for the protection of the individual's rights. It is premature, short of a more extensive test of the effectiveness of the disclosure approach as a means of assuring standards of fiducial responsibility, to make a recommendation for a regulatory agency to act as guardian for the collective interests of employees and their beneficiaries.

*Recommendations:*

(1) Future investments by retirement funds should be subject to a maximum limitation (perhaps 10 per cent) on the portion of a fund that may be held in stock or obligations of the employer company or its affiliates, regardless of the ability of such investment to meet a fiducial test.

(2) The Welfare and Pension Plans Disclosure Act should be amended by requiring the disclosure of additional information related to the investment holdings and activities of retirement plans.

## Further Study and Research

*Conclusion:*

The pension and welfare areas deserve greater emphasis in the planning of the Federal Government's research and statistical programs. Several suggestions are made for further research regarding private retirement plans.

APPENDIX C

# Actuarial Techniques

A discussion of accounting for pension costs requires as a foundation a general understanding of the techniques actuaries use in working with pension plans. This appendix is intended to provide such an understanding; it is not intended as a complete exposition of the subject matter or as an incursion into the field of technical actuarial literature. To avoid involvement in the accounting issues, this appendix will deal with actuarial techniques only as they are applied in providing information which employers may use when making *financial* provision, as opposed to *accounting* provision, for pension benefits. The acceptability of the techniques for accounting use is discussed elsewhere in this research study (see Chapter 3).

## FUNDING INSTRUMENTS AND FUNDING AGENCIES

Some pension plans stipulate that the employer will make financial provision for (fund) the benefits which are to become payable to employees upon retirement. Even when the plan is silent, the employer may decide to fund. In either event, the employer must choose—if not specified in the plan—a *funding instrument* (for example: a life insurance or annuity contract or a trust agreement) and a *funding agency* (for example: a specific life insurance company or a specific trust fund administered by a corporate or individual trustee). In some cases, two or more types of funding instruments (and, perhaps, two or more funding agencies) are used in combination. It is not necessary, for the purposes of this appendix, to discuss funding agencies further. It is essential, however, to consider funding instruments because the choice of instrument may commit the employer to the use of a specific actuarial method for determining the periodic outlay of cash.

## Contracts with Life Insurance Companies

When a life insurance company provides the funding instrument, the pension plan is known as an *insured plan.* One class of insured plan uses contracts in which premiums and benefits are determined for each covered employee. Under one such arrangement, the insurance company issues an *individual policy or policies* for each employee, usually to a trustee. Another form of arrangement in this class is a *group annuity contract*, issued to the employer. (Both individual and group contracts may provide death benefits in addition to retirement benefits.) Each of these types of arrangement specifies the premiums to be paid by the employer and the benefits to be paid to participants.

In the other class of insured arrangement, amounts contributed by the employer are not identified with specific employees until they retire. One such arrangement is called a *deposit administration contract* (or, more explicitly, a *deposit administration group annuity contract).* The insurance company keeps a separate account of the funds contributed by the employer and adds interest at an agreed rate, which is subject to change at intervals (typically five years). When an employee retires, the insurance company issues an annuity which will provide the benefits stipulated in the pension plan and transfers the single premium for the annuity from the employer's account. The premium rates for annuities are stated in the deposit administration contract. These rates, like the interest rates, are subject to change at intervals (again, typically five years). The insurance company usually makes charges for its expenses only through the annuity premiums. Periodic dividends based on experienced expenses, mortality and investment earnings are credited to the employer.

A similar type of funding instrument is the *immediate participation guarantee contract,* which differs from a deposit administration contract principally in the treatment of expenses, mortality and investment earnings. Expenses are charged directly to the employer's account, rather than through annuity premiums as they are under a deposit administration contract; mortality among retired employees affects the employer's cost immediately, rather than at intervals; annual investment earnings credits are based on the insurance company's experience, rather than on a guaranteed rate.

## Trust Agreements

When the funding instrument is a *trust agreement* and the funding agency a *trust fund,* the pension plan is called a *trust fund plan.* Under this type of arrangement, the employer's payments are made to a trustee. The trustee invests the funds in accordance with the terms of the trust agreement and either pays retirement benefits from the accumulated funds or purchases annuities from such funds for employees who retire. The trustee may be a bank or trust company, or an individual or individuals. Depending upon the terms of the trust agreement, the trustee may have sole discretion in investing the trust funds or may be subject to the general direction of the employer in making investments. Ordinarily, the trustee accepts the instructions of the employer as to the beneficiaries who should receive payments under the plan and in what amounts.

### PENSION PLAN VALUATIONS

Actuaries call the process by which they determine the amounts an employer is to contribute (pay, fund) under a pension plan (except where an insured arrangement calls for payment of specified premiums) an *actuarial valuation* of the plan. A valuation is made as of a specific date, which need not coincide with the end of the period for which a payment based on the valuation will be made. Indeed, it is uncommon for such a coincidence of dates to exist. Among other factors, a time lag is necessary in order to compile the data and to permit the actuary to make the necessary calculations. Although annual valuations are, perhaps, the rule, some employers have valuations made at less frequent intervals, in some cases as infrequently as every five years. In making valuations, actuaries ordinarily work with information—for example, the sex, date of birth, employment date and compensation of each employee covered by the plan—furnished by the employer.

Three principal concepts underlie the valuation of a pension plan:

> The calculations are made for a closed group—ordinarily, employees presently covered by the plan, former employees having vested rights and retired employees currently receiving benefits. It is recognized that a subsequent valuation may be expected to produce different results, even in the absence of a change in any other factors, because the composition of the group will have changed.
>
> The purpose is to determine the cost of benefits which will consist primarily of payments to be made over varying periods of time in the future to employees after retirement. Consequently, the ultimate cost is expressed in terms of the *present value*, as of the date of the valuation, of the expected future benefit payments. The present value is the amount which, if invested at the date of the valuation at a stated ·rate of interest, would provide the benefits expected to become payable.[1]
>
> The resulting determinations are merely estimates, since in making a valuation actuaries must tentatively resolve a number of significant uncertainties concerning future events. In doing so, they use factors called *actuarial assumptions*. Although these assumptions do not affect the actual (ultimate) cost of the plan, they have an important effect on present estimates of the cost.

## ACTUARIAL ASSUMPTIONS

The uncertainties with which actuaries must deal in estimating the cost of a pension plan relate to interest (return on funds invested),

---

[1] In pension plan valuations, actuaries combine arithmetic probability factors (examples are factors for future compensation levels, mortality, withdrawal) bearing on the amounts of benefits expected to become payable with arithmetic factors representing interest. Consequently, to actuaries, determining the present value of future pension benefits means applying factors of both types.

to expenses of administration and to the amounts and timing of benefits to be paid to presently retired employees and to present employees who will retire in the future.

## Interest (Return on Funds Invested)

The rate of interest used in an actuarial valuation is an expression of the average rate of earnings that can be expected on the funds invested or to be invested to provide for the future benefits. Since in most instances the investments include equity securities as well as debt securities, the earnings include dividends as well as interest; gains and losses on investments are also a factor. For simplicity, however, the rate is ordinarily called the *interest rate*.

In choosing the interest rate, actuaries may be influenced by the judgment of the employer or, in appropriate instances, on that of the pension plan trustee. The importance of the interest assumption is shown by the estimate that in a typical plan a variation of one-fourth of one per cent in the interest assumption can be expected to produce a differential of 6 per cent or 7 per cent in the present value of the future benefits (the higher the interest rate assumed, the lower the present value). An important factor in determining the rate of earnings is the treatment of unrealized gains or losses on investments. The method of handling these will be considered in a later section of this appendix.

## Expenses of Administration

In many instances the expenses of administering a pension plan—for example, fees of attorneys, actuaries and trustees, and the cost of keeping pension records—are borne directly by the employer. In other cases, such expenses, or some of them, are paid by a trust or insurance company from funds contributed by the employer. In the latter cases, expenses to be incurred in the future must be considered in estimating the employer's pension cost.

## Benefits

Several assumptions must be made as to the amounts and timing of the future benefits whose present value is used in expressing the cost of a pension plan. The principal assumptions are discussed in the following paragraphs.

*Future compensation levels*

Benefits under some pension plans depend in part on future compensation levels. For example, the annual retirement benefit may be a stated percentage, for each year of service, of the employee's average compensation for the final five or ten years of employment. Under plans of this type, provision is ordinarily made for normal increases arising from the progression of employees through the various earnings-rate categories, based on the employer's experience. Special provision may be made for anticipated increases in compensation of executives, whose progress does not necessarily follow the normal statistics. Provision is not specifically made, however, for general earnings-level increases, such as those which may result from inflation. (The Internal Revenue Service ordinarily does not permit such provision to be made.)

*Cost-of-living*

In order to protect the purchasing power of retirement benefits, some plans provide that the benefits otherwise determined will be adjusted from time to time to reflect variations in a specific index, such as the Consumer Price Index of the United States Bureau of Labor Statistics. In estimating the cost of such a plan, actuaries must make provision for expected changes in the cost-of-living index.

*Mortality*

The length of time an employee covered by a pension plan will live is a determining factor in the amount and timing of the benefit payments he will receive. If an employee dies before he becomes eligible for pension benefits, he receives no payments (although in some plans his beneficiaries receive lump-sum or periodic benefits). The total amount of pension benefits for employees who reach retirement is determined in large part by how long they live thereafter.

While the ultimate amount of pension benefits will depend on the actual mortality, actuaries must rely on mortality tables in estimating future pension payments. In spite of the fact that mortality tables are constructed with mathematical precision and represent the experience of large numbers of lives, their use in pension plan valuations does not imply an equivalent degree of precision in the resulting estimates of pension payments. In fact, actuaries must exercise a high degree of judgment in selecting and using mortality tables, since mortality varies by group, for many reasons.

Actuaries have several devices for coping with the variations. For example, special mortality tables have been developed for annuitants, based on successively more recent experience. Among annuity tables in use are those designated 1937, 1949 and 1951.[2] The 1949 and 1951 tables recognized the factor of expected improvement in longevity, using a technique called a *projection scale*. Improvement in longevity may also be recognized by making a *set-back* of ages, sometimes in conjunction with one of several available projections of a table. In making a set-back, actuaries apply a mortality table as if each employee in the calculation were one or more years younger than he actually is. Set-backs are often used for women employees because of their greater life expectancy. The effect of a variation in the mortality assumption is illustrated by the estimate that a one-year set-back in ages can be expected to increase the present value of the future pension benefits by approximately 4 per cent.

*Retirement age*

Most plans provide a normal retirement age, but many plans permit employees to work thereafter under certain conditions. Some plans provide for retirement in advance of the normal age in case of disability, and most plans permit early retirement at the employee's option under certain conditions. When there are such provisions, actuaries must estimate their effect on the amount and timing of the benefits which will ultimately be paid.

*Withdrawal (turnover)*

In many plans, an employee who leaves the employer for any reason other than retirement forfeits his right to receive benefits. In estimating the amount of future benefits, actuaries may make allowance for the effect of withdrawal (turnover).

---

[2] These tables, based on experience for a number of years prior to the years specified, are known, more precisely, as the "1937 Standard Annuity Table," the "Annuity Table for 1949," and the "Group Annuity Table for 1951," respectively.

*Vesting*

Many plans provide that after a stated number of years of service an employee becomes entitled to receive benefits (commencing at his normal retirement age and usually varying in amount with his number of years of service) even though he leaves the company for a reason other than retirement. This must be taken into consideration in estimating the effect of withdrawal.

*Social security benefits*

For plans which provide that pensions otherwise payable are to be reduced by all or part of social security benefits, it is necessary in estimating future pension benefits to estimate future social security benefits. Ordinarily, this estimate is based on the assumption that such benefits will remain at the level in effect at the time the valuation is being made.

## Actuarial Gains and Losses

Regardless of the actuary's degree of skill, the likelihood that actual events will coincide with each of the assumptions used is so remote as to constitute an impossibility. As a result, the actuarial assumptions used may be changed from time to time as experience and judgment dictate. In addition, whether or not the assumptions as to events in the future are changed, it is often necessary to recognize in the calculations the effect of differences between actual prior experience and the assumptions used in the past. If the assumptions in use have been unduly pessimistic, the adjustments which result are *actuarial gains;* if the assumptions have been unduly optimistic, the adjustments are *actuarial losses.* The net effect of the gains and losses determined in a particular valuation is ordinarily dealt with as a single amount.

There are two techniques for recognizing the adjustment. The *immediate basis* (not ordinarily used for net losses) applies net gains in determining the next contribution made to the funding agency after the adjustment is determined. The *spread basis* applies a net gain or loss to current and future contributions, either through the normal cost or through the past service cost. In some funding calculations, the immediate basis is used for net actuarial gains, while the spread basis is used for net losses.

# FUNDING METHODS[3]

When a decision has been made to fund the cost of a pension plan, and a funding instrument and funding agency have been chosen, a specific funding method must be selected for use in determining the amounts of the periodic payments to the funding agency (unless the payments are stated premiums). As the discussion in this section will show, the choice of a certain type of funding instrument may also require commitment to a specific funding method; with some types of

---

[3] The Committee on Pension and Profit-Sharing Terminology of The American Risk and Insurance Association has proposed the expression *actuarial cost method* to replace the expression *funding method*, used in the past. The Committee has also proposed new classifications and terminology for actuarial cost methods. The proposed new terminology is compared below with the related terms most commonly employed in present practice and used in this study:

| *Proposed new terminology* | *Terms used in this study* |
|---|---|
| Accrued benefit cost method | Unit credit method |
| Projected benefit cost methods: | |
|   Individual level cost methods: | |
|     Without supplemental liability | Individual level premium method |
|     With supplemental liability | Entry age normal method (individual basis) |
|   Aggregate level cost methods: | |
|     Without supplemental liability | Aggregate method |
|     With supplemental liability | Attained age normal method; entry age normal method (aggregate basis) |
| Supplemental liability | Past service cost; prior service cost |

It should be noted that the *pay-as-you-go* procedure and *terminal funding*, discussed in this appendix, are not actuarial cost methods because they do not make provision for future retirement benefits during employees' periods of active service. It should be noted that the word "level," as used in the new terminology, refers to the cost recognized for each participant in successive periods, rather than to the employer's total cost for the periods. Initial conclusions of the terminology committee were presented in an article entitled "Actuarial Cost Methods—New Pension Terminology," by Joseph J. Melone, in *The Journal of Insurance*, Sept. 1963, pp. 456-464. A more detailed analysis of the new classifications and terminology may be found in Dan M. McGill's *Fundamentals of Private Pensions*, Second Edition, 1961, pp. 219-238.

funding instruments, however, the employer has wide latitude in choosing a funding method.

Although funding methods are alike in that they invoke the same general concepts and use actuarial assumptions, they differ significantly in their approach and can produce widely varying results. In addition, there are different ways of proceeding under the various methods. Because of the number and complexity of possible variations, the discussion following should be viewed as illustrative rather than comprehensive.

The results derived under the principal methods in use are compared in Table I (pages 124-125), which is based on a table published as part of a paper prepared by Charles L. Trowbridge in 1952.[4]

The calculations underlying the table are based on a hypothetical employee group. At the inception of the plan, none of the employees has retired. As employees retire and are replaced, the group approaches maturity—a condition in which the age distribution, including the ages of employees who have retired, approximates a distribution which is expected to be duplicated year after year. If this condition were reached or approximated, the annual contribution (payment) under any particular funding method would remain the same or approximately so. This theoretical result is represented in Table I by the entries under "Contribution," captioned "Limit." (The assumption of an initially immature group of employees is applicable to pension plans recently adopted and to plans of employers whose operations are growing. In both instances, the proportion of pensioners to active employees is low in relation to the proportion represented by the theoretical condition of maturity.) Other assumptions in Table I (which was calculated in 1952) are an interest rate of 2.5 per cent and a retirement benefit of $420 annually. The past service cost, when developed under a particular funding method, has been amortized in the table over a period of twenty years. Changes in the conditions and assumptions specified would, of course, vary the amounts appearing in the table, but the trend indicated would remain.

## Pay-As-You-Go

*Pay-as-you-go* is not truly a funding method because funding as applied to pension plans connotes making financial provision for pen-

---

[4] "Fundamentals of Pension Funding," *Transactions of the Society of Actuaries*, Volume IV, 1952, pp. 17-43.

sion benefits *before* they become payable. In pay-as-you-go, no payments are made until the benefits themselves are paid. As Table I shows, the payments under this method increase substantially as more and more employees receive retirement benefits.

## Terminal Funding

In *terminal funding,* advance financial provision *is* made for future pension obligations, but only at the end (hence the word "terminal") of an employee's period of active service. At that time the employer either purchases a single-premium annuity which will provide the retirement benefit or makes an actuarially equivalent contribution to a trust. As in the case of pay-as-you-go, payments under terminal funding start at a relatively low level, increase as more employees retire under the plan, and level out as the group matures. In terminal funding, however, the rate of increase is less marked because of the element of advance provision for benefits. In addition, since the payments under this method, whether made to an insurance company or to a trust, exceed the retirement benefits immediately due, a fund is created. Part of the cost of paying pensions is met by earnings of the fund.

An employer purchasing annuities under the terminal funding method may have actuarial gains in the form of dividends. If payments are made to a trust, either gains or losses may arise in relation to either mortality or fund earnings. Ordinarily, under the terminal funding method, actuarial gains and losses are recognized on the immediate basis (that is, by reducing or increasing the next payment made after they are determined).

Terminal funding is often used in plans, such as those negotiated with unions, which require only that pensions be provided for employees retiring during a specified period. This method may, however, be used with other types of plans.

## Unit Credit Method

Under the *unit credit method* (new terminology: *accrued benefit cost method*[5]), future service benefits (pension benefits based on service after the inception of a plan) are funded as they accrue—that is, as each employee works out the service period involved (hence the

---

[5] See footnote [3] on page 121 for a discussion of proposed new terminology.

## Table I*

### Comparison of Results Under

|  | Pay-as-you-go† | Terminal funding† | Unit credit method — Past service cost funded over 20 years | Unit credit method — Past service cost funded as to interest only |
|---|---|---|---|---|
| Past service cost | $ — | $ — | $ 431,924 | $431,924 |
| Initial normal cost | — | — | 26,371 | 26,371 |
| Ultimate normal cost | — | — | 33,563 | 33,563 |
| **Contribution—beginning of year** | | | | |
| 1 | — | — | 53,402 | 36,906 |
| 2 | 840 | 10,151 | 54,398 | 37,902 |
| 3 | 2,100 | 15,226 | 55,267 | 38,771 |
| 4 | 3,543 | 18,456 | 56,058 | 39,562 |
| 5 | 5,326 | 23,070 | 56,731 | 40,234 |
| 10 | 17,270 | 39,041 | 58,821 | 42,324 |
| 15 | 30,006 | 42,295 | 59,933 | 43,437 |
| 20 | 40,582 | 44,134 | 60,863 | 44,367 |
| 21 | 42,356 | 44,409 | 34,008 | 44,543 |
| 25 | 48,158 | 45,316 | 34,694 | 45,229 |
| 30 | 54,443 | 55,829 | 34,934 | 45,468 |
| 35 | 62,999 | 63,442 | 33,480 | 44,014 |
| 40 | 65,559 | 50,369 | 33,077 | 43,612 |
| 50 | 64,249 | 49,227 | 33,388 | 43,923 |
| Limit | 63,000 | 50,753 | 33,563 | 44,098 |
| **Fund balance—end of year** | | | | |
| 1 | — | — | 54,737 | 37,829 |
| 2 | — | 9,543 | 111,002 | 76,762 |
| 3 | — | 23,236 | 168,273 | 116,269 |
| 4 | — | 39,103 | 226,307 | 156,094 |
| 5 | — | 58,267 | 284,655 | 195,777 |
| 10 | — | 178,161 | 569,997 | 380,564 |
| 15 | — | 288,992 | 831,283 | 528,079 |
| 20 | — | 364,714 | 1,070,060 | 638,136 |
| 21 | — | 375,937 | 1,088,255 | 656,331 |
| 25 | — | 410,149 | 1,151,480 | 719,556 |
| 30 | — | 454,999 | 1,213,230 | 781,305 |
| 35 | — | 528,172 | 1,235,435 | 803,511 |
| 40 | — | 536,121 | 1,225,500 | 793,576 |
| 50 | — | 501,002 | 1,202,048 | 770,124 |
| Limit | — | 502,104 | 1,206,924 | 775,000 |

Notes:

* Adapted from a table appearing in "Fundamentals of Pension Funding," by Charles L. Trowbridge, *Transactions of the Society of Actuaries*, Volume IV, 1952, p. 36. The assumptions underlying the calculations are discussed on page 122.

† Pay-as-you-go and terminal funding are not considered to be "actuarial cost methods"; the results under these procedures are included in the table for comparative purposes.

APPENDIX C: ACTUARIAL TECHNIQUES

## Various Methods of Funding Pension Cost†

| Entry age normal method ||||| Attained age normal method ||
|---|---|---|---|---|---|---|
| Past service cost funded over 20 years | Past service cost funded as to interest only | Individual level premium method | Aggregate method || Past service cost funded over 20 years | Past service cost funded as to interest only |
| 661,315 | $661,315 | $ — § | $ — § || $ 431,924 | $ 431,924 |
| 27,101 | 27,101 | — § | — § || 50,858 | 50,858 |
| 27,101 | 27,101 | — § | — § || 27,101 | 27,101 |
| | | | | | | |
| 68,488 | 43,230 | 126,488 | 95,591 || 77,889 | 61,393 |
| 68,488 | 43,230 | 112,387 | 89,867 || 75,903 | 59,407 |
| 68,488 | 43,230 | 101,472 | 84,685 || 74,106 | 57,610 |
| 68,488 | 43,230 | 92,778 | 79,995 || 72,479 | 55,983 |
| 68,488 | 43,230 | 85,061 | 75,728 || 70,999 | 54,503 |
| 68,488 | 43,230 | 57,235 | 59,233 || 65,277 | 48,781 |
| 68,488 | 43,230 | 42,032 | 43,331 || 61,484 | 44,988 |
| 68,488 | 43,230 | 34,060 | 37,730 || 58,947 | 42,451 |
| 27,101 | 43,230 | 33,002 | 36,858 || 31,521 | 42,056 |
| 27,101 | 43,230 | 29,971 | 34,015 || 30,233 | 40,768 |
| 27,101 | 43,230 | 27,900 | 31,568 || 29,125 | 39,660 |
| 27,101 | 43,230 | 27,101 | 29,949 || 28,391 | 38,926 |
| 27,101 | 43,230 | 27,101 | 28,930 || 27,929 | 38,464 |
| 27,101 | 43,230 | 27,101 | 27,867 || 27,448 | 37,983 |
| 27,101 | 43,230 | 27,101 | 27,101 || 27,101 | 37,636 |
| | | | | | | |
| 70,200 | 44,311 | 129,651 | 97,981 || 79,836 | 62,928 |
| 141,293 | 88,869 | 247,228 | 191,683 || 158,772 | 124,532 |
| 212,873 | 133,249 | 355,265 | 281,125 || 236,547 | 184,543 |
| 284,763 | 177,260 | 455,613 | 366,515 || 313,120 | 242,907 |
| 356,622 | 220,543 | 548,731 | 447,840 || 388,263 | 299,385 |
| 707,342 | 417,303 | 918,561 | 794,067 || 737,424 | 547,991 |
| ,035,096 | 570,864 | 1,160,817 | 1,090,139 || 1,039,107 | 735,903 |
| ,343,743 | 682,428 | 1,315,868 | 1,251,691 || 1,302,039 | 870,115 |
| ,361,700 | 700,385 | 1,339,177 | 1,277,347 || 1,323,484 | 891,560 |
| ,422,100 | 760,785 | 1,413,822 | 1,362,729 || 1,395,201 | 963,277 |
| ,476,931 | 815,616 | 1,475,905 | 1,438,799 || 1,459,655 | 1,027,731 |
| ,495,910 | 834,594 | 1,495,910 | 1,471,378 || 1,484,796 | 1,052,872 |
| ,487,884 | 826,569 | 1,487,884 | 1,472,026 || 1,480,699 | 1,048,775 |
| ,467,601 | 806,286 | 1,467,601 | 1,460,955 || 1,464,588 | 1,032,664 |
| ,471,873 | 810,558 | 1,471,873 | 1,471,873 || 1,471,873 | 1,039,949 |

† See footnote [3] on page 121 for a discussion of proposed new terminology.

§ Past service cost and normal cost are not determined separately under either the individual level premium method or the aggregate method. The annual contributions under these methods include amortization (not separately identified) of past service cost.

"accrued" in *accrued benefit*). Thus, the normal cost under this method for a particular year is the present value of the units of future benefit credited to employees for service in that year (hence *unit credit*).

As an example, if a plan provides benefits of $4 per month for each year of credited service, the normal cost for a particular employee for a particular year is the present value (usually adjusted for withdrawal and for mortality before retirement) of an annuity of $4 per month beginning at the employee's anticipated retirement date and continuing throughout his life. In some plans, a single-premium annuity is purchased for each employee each year in an amount determined in the manner just described. (For this reason, the unit credit funding method is sometimes called the *single-premium method.*)

The past service cost under the unit credit method, like the normal cost, is the present value of a unit of benefits—that is, the value at the inception of the plan of the pension benefits based on employee service prior to the date of inception.

The annual payment to the funding agency under the unit credit method ordinarily comprises (1) the normal cost and (2) an amount for past service cost. The latter may comprise only interest or may also include an amount intended to reduce the unfunded balance. The actuary ordinarily calculates (a) the minimum and maximum payments conforming to regulations of the Internal Revenue Service and (b) a payment on the basis chosen by the employer, if different from the Internal Revenue Service minimum or maximum. In general, the minimum payment necessary to meet Internal Revenue Service requirements for maintaining a plan in a qualified status is an amount equal to the normal cost plus interest, at the rate on which the actuarial calculations for the plan are based, on the unfunded prior service cost at the beginning of the year. If more than this minimum is paid in some year or years, however, the actual minimum in some later year or years may be correspondingly reduced, perhaps to zero. The maximum is the normal cost, less any net actuarial gain, plus one-tenth of the initial past service cost. Since there is not a separate allowance for interest, the shortest period for amortizing past service cost by tax-deductible installment payments is approximately twelve years.

Thus, the impact of the unit credit method on the employer's financial statements depends on the employer's policy in dealing with past service cost. Table I illustrates the effect of two of the available choices—funding only an amount equal to interest on past service cost and funding the entire amount over a period of twenty years. As Table I shows, at the outset, the annual contributions under either of these choices gradually increase, ultimately declining as they approach the theoretical limit. Several factors account generally for these trends. As to individual employees, the annual normal cost of the plan increases each year because the period to the employee's retirement continually shortens while the annual unit of benefit remains constant. (For this reason the unit credit method is sometimes called the *step-rate method.*) As to the employees collectively, however, this step-up effect is masked, since older employees generating the highest annual cost are continually replaced by new employees generating the lowest. For a mature employee group, the normal cost would be the same each year. In the illustration in Table I, the annual normal cost increases as the group approaches maturity. This increase is offset, and eventually overcome, by earnings on the accumulating pension fund.

Net actuarial gains under the unit credit method are ordinarily recognized on the immediate basis—that is, by reducing the maximum payment to the funding agency for the period following the date of the actuarial valuation in which the gain is determined. (This is due in large part to a requirement of the Internal Revenue Service.) Net actuarial losses under the unit credit method are ordinarily added to the unfunded past service cost.

The unit credit method is almost always used when the funding instrument is a group annuity contract and may also be used in trusteed plans and with deposit administration contracts—commonly for plans in which the benefit is a stated amount per year of service, infrequently for plans which provide a fixed benefit (for example, $100 per month) or benefits based on earnings of a future period. (The "unit of benefit" under formulas of the latter type is not clearly identified and must be determined on an arbitrary basis if the unit credit method is applied.)

## Entry Age Normal Method

As the foregoing discussion explained, the unit credit method assigns only the cost of benefits which have *accrued* (in the limited sense that the units of employee service on which benefits are based have been rendered). By contrast, the other actuarial cost methods look forward. That is, they apportion to past, present and future periods the entire cost of an employee's *projected* benefits, without regard to the periods during which the service on which the benefits are based has been or will be rendered. Perhaps the most frequently used method in the latter group is the *entry age normal method*. It assumes (1) that every employee entered the plan (thus, *entry age*) at the time of employment or at the earliest time he would have been eligible if the plan had then been in existence and (2) that contributions have been made on this basis from the entry age to the date of the actuarial valuation (the contributions are level annual amounts which, if accumulated at the interest rate used in the actuarial valuation, would at the time of the employee's retirement equal the then present value of his pension). Ordinarily, the assumptions are a fiction because most plans were established after the employer had been in existence for some time. Had the assumption been true, however, a fund would have been created and would have grown through accumulation of earnings. The amount of the theoretical fund at the date of inception of the plan is the amount of the past service cost under this method.

*Aggregate basis*

In theory, the normal cost payments under the entry age normal method are level amounts for each employee such that, if the amounts were paid annually over each employee's entire period of recognized service, funds would be available at his retirement date to provide in full for his pension. However, when the *entry age normal method* is applied on the *aggregate basis* (new terminology: *aggregate level cost method with supplemental liability*[6]), separate amounts are not determined for individual employees. Further departures of practice from theory often encountered are (1) the use of an average entry age and (2) the use, particularly when benefits are based on employees' earnings, of a level percentage of payroll in determining annual payments. In other types of plans, the normal cost contribution rate may be a flat amount per employee, or the normal cost contribution itself may be a flat amount. The following illustrates, in simplified, summary form, a typical procedure for the first valuation of a pension plan, using the percentage method (for simplicity, benefit payments have been ignored).

---

[6] See footnote [3] on page 121 for a discussion of proposed new terminology.

As of theoretical eligibility dates:
(a) Present value of future pension benefits (participants
    at inception) $ 200,000
(b) Present value of future compensation (participants at
    inception) 5,000,000
(c) Contribution rate for normal cost (a) ÷ (b) 4.00%

As of the inception date of the plan:
(d) Present value of future pension benefits (participants at
    inception) $ 270,000
(e) Present value of future compensation (participants at
    inception) 4,250,000
(f) Present value of future normal cost contributions
    (e) × (c) 170,000
(g) Past service cost (d) − (f) 100,000

For the first year of the plan:
(h) Actual compensation of covered employees 225,000
(i) Normal cost (h) × (c) 9,000
(j) Payment for past service cost (assuming amortization
    over 20 years) 6,700
(k) Contribution for the year (i) + (j) 15,700

In valuations for succeeding years, the past service cost is usually *frozen* (that is, changed only to recognize payments and the accrual of interest), although a new past service cost may be determined each year, generally on the basis indicated above. If the past service cost is frozen, actuarial gains and losses are spread into the future, entering into the normal cost for future years. The same would be true of the effect of a change in plan benefits such as might occur if the plan were amended subsequent to its adoption. If, on the other hand, a new past service cost is determined, the amount includes the effects, for years prior to the date of the valuation being made, of actuarial gains and losses and changes in plan benefits. The following carries the foregoing illustration into the second year, assuming that past service cost is to be frozen.

As of the second valuation date:
(a) Present value of future pension benefits (participants
    at second valuation date) $ 280,000
(b) Amount in pension fund (initial contribution of $15,700
    plus earnings) 16,000
(c) Remaining cost (a) − (b) 264,000
    Unfunded past service cost:
(d)   Amount at inception of plan 100,000
(e)   Interest for one year 3,000
(f)   (d) + (e) 103,000

|   |   |   |
|---|---|---|
| | Less: | |
| (g) | Contribution for past service | 6,700 |
| (h) | Interest (assuming payment at midyear) | 100 |
| (i) | (g) + (h) | 6,800 |
| (j) | Unfunded past service cost (f) − (i) | 96,200 |
| (k) | Present value of future contributions for normal cost (c) − (j) | 167,800 |
| (l) | Present value of future compensation (participants at second valuation date) | 4,150,000 |
| (m) | Contribution rate for normal cost (k) ÷ (l) | 4.04% |

For the second year of the plan:
| | | |
|---|---|---|
| (n) | Actual compensation of covered employees | $ 220,000 |
| (o) | Normal cost contribution (n) × (m) | 8,888 |
| (p) | Payment for past service cost (assuming amortization over 20 years) | 6,700 |
| (q) | Contribution for the year (o) + (p) | 15,588 |

*Individual basis*

When the *entry age normal method* is applied on the *individual basis* (new terminology: *individual level cost method with supplemental liability*[7]), the theory is generally the same, but the calculations are made for individuals, rather than for the covered employees as a group. The effects, for years prior to a valuation, of actuarial gains and losses and changes in plan benefits enter into the determination of unfunded past service cost.

*Other considerations*

Regardless of the basis used in applying the entry age normal method, the annual contribution to the funding agency, as shown in the examples, comprises the normal cost and an amount for the past service cost (interest only, or interest plus amortization of principal). The considerations in determining the past service payment are in general the same as those for the unit credit funding method.

Table I shows that the entry age normal method generates annual payments which are exactly equal, except for a reduction when the past service cost has been fully funded. This is because the pension benefit in the hypothetical plan on which the table is based is an unvarying amount. Had the benefit been based in part on years of service or on employee earnings, the annual normal cost contributions

---

[7] See footnote [3] on page 121 for a discussion of proposed new terminology.

would probably have been based either on a flat amount per employee or on a percentage of compensation. In either event, the annual amounts would have tended to vary somewhat but would nonetheless have been substantially level. Since the calculations are based on the entire period of service of covered employees, the annual payment is not affected by changes in the composition of the group as it matures. The entry age normal method creates the largest fund of any of the methods thus far considered; consequently the ultimate annual normal payment under this method is lower than the ultimate annual payments under any of the other such methods.

The entry age normal method is often used when the funding instrument is a trust agreement or a deposit administration contract.

## Individual Level Premium Method

The *individual level premium method* (new terminology: *individual level cost method without supplemental liability*[8]) assigns the cost of each employee's pension, in level annual amounts or as a level percentage of the employee's compensation, over the period from the date of his entry into the plan (for a new plan, the inception date) to his retirement. Past service cost is not determined separately under the individual level premium method.

The individual level premium method is most commonly used when the funding instrument consists of individual insurance or annuity policies. It may be used, however, in trusteed plans and with deposit administration contracts.

In plans using individual annuity policies, the employer is protected against actuarial losses, since premiums paid are not ordinarily subject to retroactive increases. The insurance company may, however, pass part of any actuarial gains along to the employer by means of dividends. Employee turnover may be another source of actuarial gains under such insured plans, since all or part of the cash surrender values of policies previously purchased for employees leaving the employer for reasons other than retirement may revert to the company (or to the trust). Dividends and cash surrender values are ordinarily used to reduce the premiums payable for the next period; thus, the actuarial gains are recognized on the immediate basis. In using the individual level premium method for trust fund plans, actuarial gains and losses are ordinarily recognized on the spread basis.

---

[8] *Ibid.*

As Table I shows, the individual level premium method generates annual costs which are initially very high and which ultimately drop to the level of the normal cost determined under the entry age normal method. The high initial costs arise because the past service cost (although not separately identified) for employees near retirement when the plan is adopted is in effect amortized over a very short period.

## Aggregate Method

The *aggregate method* (new terminology: *aggregate level cost method without supplemental liability*[9]) applies on a collective basis the principle followed for individuals in the individual level premium method. That is, the entire unfunded cost of future pension benefits (including benefits to be paid to employees who have retired as of the date of the valuation) is spread over the average future working period (service lives) of employees who are active as of the date of the valuation. In most cases this is done by the use of a percentage of payroll. The following illustrates, for the first and second years of a plan, the procedure typically followed in applying the aggregate method (for simplicity, benefit payments have been ignored).

|  | First year of plan | Second year of plan |
|---|---|---|
| As of the valuation date: | | |
| (a) Present value of future pension benefits (participants at valuation date) | $ 270,000 | $ 280,000 |
| (b) Amount in pension fund (initial contribution of $14,300 plus earnings) | — | 14,600 |
| (c) Remaining cost (a) − (b) | 270,000 | 265,400 |
| (d) Present value of future compensation (participants at valuation date) | 4,250,000 | 4,150,000 |
| (e) Aggregate cost contribution rate (c) ÷ (d) | 6.35% | 6.40% |
| For the year: | | |
| (f) Actual compensation of covered employees | $ 225,000 | $ 220,000 |
| (g) Contribution for the year (f) × (e) | 14,300 | 14,100 |

As the foregoing illustration shows, the aggregate method does not deal separately with past service cost. As the illustration also shows, actuarial gains and losses enter into the determination of the contribution rate and, consequently, are spread over future periods (under this

---

[9] See footnote [3] on page 121 for a discussion of proposed new terminology.

method, it would be extremely difficult to isolate the effect either of changes in actuarial assumptions or of deviations between actual experience and assumptions used).

As shown in Table I, annual contributions under the aggregate method decrease, but the rate of decrease is less extreme than under the individual level premium method. The aggregate cost method amortizes past service cost (not separately identified) over the average remaining service lives of participants, thus avoiding the very short individual amortization periods of the individual level premium method.

The aggregate method may be modified by introducing past service cost. If the past service cost is determined by the entry age normal method, the modified aggregate method is the same as the entry age normal method applied on the aggregate basis (page 128). If the past service cost is determined by the unit credit method, the modified aggregate method is called the attained age normal method (discussed below).

The aggregate method is used principally with trust fund plans and with plans funded under deposit administration contracts.

## Attained Age Normal Method

The *attained age normal method* (new terminology: *aggregate level cost method with supplemental liability*[10]) is a variant of the aggregate method in which past service cost, determined at the inception of the plan under the unit credit method, is recognized separately. The cost of each employee's benefits assigned to years after the inception of the plan is spread over the employee's remaining service life. Normal cost contributions under the attained age normal method, usually determined as a percentage of payroll, tend to decline but less markedly than under the aggregate method.

As with the unit credit and entry age normal methods, the past service cost may be amortized in a variety of ways, or may not be funded at all, in which case it is customary to fund an amount equivalent to interest.

This method is used in trust fund plans and in plans funded under deposit administration contracts.

---

[10] *Ibid.*

# UNREALIZED APPRECIATION (DEPRECIATION) OF PENSION FUND INVESTMENTS

The discussion of actuarial assumptions in an earlier section of this appendix showed that the earnings of a pension fund, entering into actuarial calculations through the "interest assumption," may be a composite of interest, dividends, real estate earnings and other types of income, and that profits or losses when securities or other assets are sold are also a factor influencing actual earnings. Actual earnings inevitably vary from the interest assumption, giving rise to actuarial gains or losses. These *experienced* gains or losses arise whether or not the actuarial assumption as to future fund earnings is revised, and they are ordinarily given effect when determined.

If the amount of the pension fund enters directly into the calculation of pension cost, as it does under some actuarial cost methods, experienced gains and losses may reduce or increase either (1) the normal cost for the present year and future years (the *spread basis*) or (2) any unfunded prior service cost (*a spread basis* if such cost is amortized). In other instances, the entire amount of a net experienced gain or loss is applied to reduce or increase the employer's contribution for the year after it is determined (the *immediate basis*). With either type of actuarial cost method, it must be decided whether to recognize *unrealized* appreciation. For most pension funds, long-range depreciation of investment securities has not been a problem.

Changes in the market values of bonds are seldom recognized, primarily because bonds are ordinarily held to maturity. Under some pension plans (called *equity annuity plans*), appreciation (or depreciation) of securities in a specific portfolio is assigned to participants in order to provide a measure of protection of the purchasing power of retirement benefits. Ordinarily, such assigned appreciation (depreciation) is not taken into consideration in determining the employer's cost.

If unrealized appreciation is to be taken into consideration, any of several procedures may be used. Some valuations recognize the full market value of common stocks. In other instances, a three- or five-year moving average of market values is used. Frequently, the amount included in the calculations for common stocks is limited to a percentage (such as 80 per cent) of the market value.

When a moving average of market values is used, the purpose is to minimize the effect of short-term market fluctuations. Various other formulas may also be used for this purpose. One formula assumes long-range appreciation of 3 per cent (some employers use other percentages) annually. The formula is applied as follows:

1. Each year, 3 per cent of the average amount (cost plus appreciation previously recognized) of common stocks in the fund is added to an appreciation account.
2. The appreciation account is reduced ratably when common stocks are sold.
3. Cost and appreciation combined are not permitted to exceed a specified percentage (85 per cent is typical) of the average market value. This may serve to limit the amount of the increase in the appreciation account described in (1) above.
4. The pension fund total deducted in arriving at the present value of future contributions for normal cost includes common stocks at their cost plus the balance in the appreciation account.

Another formula assumes that the long-range return on common stock investments, including both dividends and appreciation, will be 7 per cent (some employers use other percentages) annually. The amount by which 7 per cent of the average investment in common stocks (cost plus depreciation previously recognized) exceeds dividends received during the year is added to an appreciation account and is treated as an experienced actuarial gain.

## ACTUARIES

The propriety of an employer's charge to expense for pension cost ordinarily depends at least in part on the competence and judgment of an actuary. Accordingly, a brief discussion of the actuarial profession may be useful to accountants and others.

There is at present no provision for accreditation of actuaries by governmental authority. There are, however, four actuarial organizations whose objectives and requirements for membership give some indication of the qualifications of their members. The organizations have in common the objective, among others, of maintaining high professional standards. To this end they provide guides for the professional conduct of members.

## Casualty Actuarial Society

The Casualty Actuarial Society, established in 1914, is concerned primarily with problems in the field of insurance other than life insurance. Its membership consists of approximately 210 Fellows and 180 Associates. To become an Associate, an applicant must, among other requirements, pass technical examinations conducted by the Society. To become a Fellow, an Associate must pass additional examinations.

## Conference of Actuaries in Public Practice

Members of the Conference of Actuaries in Public Practice, established in 1950, work principally with life insurance and employee benefit plans. There are approximately 130 Fellows and 200 Members. To become a Member, an applicant must, among other requirements, have had seven years of actuarial experience, not less than three of which must have been in public practice. To become a Fellow, a candidate must have had fifteen years of actuarial experience, not less than five of which must have been in public practice.

## Fraternal Actuarial Association

The Fraternal Actuarial Association, established in 1916, is concerned primarily with problems relating to insurance provided through fraternal organizations. It has approximately seventy-five Active Members and fifty Associate Members. An applicant for Associate Membership must, among other requirements, have attained mathematical proficiency at the college level or its equivalent and have had experience with fraternal insurance. To become an Active Member, an applicant must have been an Associate Member for one year, must be engaged in work in fraternal insurance, must have presented an acceptable paper to the Association, and must be a member of another actuarial organization or have had at least ten years of substantial actuarial experience, at least five of which have been related to fraternal insurance.

## Society of Actuaries

The Society of Actuaries is the oldest and largest of the several actuarial organizations. The present organization resulted from a merger in 1949 of the Actuarial Society of America (established in

1889) and the American Institute of Actuaries (established in 1909). The membership of the Society includes approximately 1,300 Fellows and 1,000 Associates. To become an Associate, a candidate must, among other requirements, pass technical examinations conducted by the Society. An Associate may become a Fellow upon passing additional examinations.

## Proposed New Association

A Joint Committee on Organization of the Actuarial Profession has developed plans for forming a new American Academy of Actuaries to serve as the basis for accreditation of actuaries in the United States. The Academy would be chartered by the Federal Government.

Certain actuaries would become members of the Academy at the time of its organization. This group would include any individual resident in the United States who at that time was a Fellow of the Casualty Actuarial Society, a Fellow of the Conference of Actuaries in Public Practice, an Active Member of the Fraternal Actuarial Association, or a Fellow of the Society of Actuaries. During an interim period, Associates (Associate Members) of these groups could become members of the Academy by meeting requirements as to experience and education and in some instances, by passing examinations conducted by the Academy. After the interim period, candidates for membership would need to comply with requirements as to experience and education and to pass comprehensive examinations testing their knowledge of subjects pertinent to actuarial work. In addition to examinations on certain general subjects, there would be more specific ones in the fields of life insurance, health insurance and pensions on the one hand or property insurance and casualty insurance on the other hand.

APPENDIX D

# Glossary

The terms listed in this glossary are defined in the way they are used in other parts of this research study. The meanings ascribed to the various terms are intended also to be the meanings the terms have in present practice. In addition, reference is made, where appropriate, to new terminology proposed by a committee of The American Risk and Insurance Association (see *actuarial cost method*).

**Accrual.** See *accrue*.

**Accrue.** In this study, when *accrue* is used in accounting discussions, it has the customary accounting meaning. When used in relation to actuarial terms or procedures, however, the intended meaning differs somewhat. When actuaries say that pension benefits, actuarial costs and actuarial liabilities have *accrued*, they ordinarily mean that the amounts are associated, either specifically or by a process of allocation, with years of employee service before the date of a particular valuation of a pension plan. Actuaries do not ordinarily intend their use of the word "accrue" to have the more conclusive accounting significance.

**Accrued Actuarial Liability.** The excess of the present value, as of the date of a pension plan valuation, of prospective pension benefits and administrative expenses over the sum of (1) the amount in the pension fund and (2) the present value of future contributions for *normal cost* determined by any of several actuarial techniques (see *actuarial cost method, funding method*). This excess is also (infrequently) called the *actuarial reserve requirement*. At the inception of a pension plan, this excess is the *past service cost;* at the date of a later valuation, the *unfunded prior service cost* (see *supplemental liability*).

**Accrued Benefit Cost Method.** See *actuarial cost method.*

**Actuarial.** Relating to the work of an *actuary.* Computations using compound interest, mortality tables, and other factors in the field of actuarial science are called *actuarial* computations.

**Actuarial Adjustment.** The net of the actuarial gains and losses recognized in an actuarial valuation. (This expression, not in general use, has been introduced in this research study to simplify the discussion of actuarial gains and losses.)

**Actuarial Assumptions.** Factors which actuaries use in tentatively resolving uncertainties concerning future events affecting pension cost. See, for example, *interest, mortality rate, withdrawal.*

**Actuarial Cost.** See *pension cost.*

**Actuarial Cost Method.** A particular technique for establishing the amount and incidence of the annual actuarial cost accrual for pension plan benefits, or benefits and expenses, and the related actuarial liability. This term and the definition have been proposed (to replace the expression *funding method,* used in the past) by the Committee on Pension and Profit-Sharing Terminology of The American Risk and Insurance Association. The Committee has also proposed new classifications and terminology for actuarial cost methods. The proposed new terminology is compared below with the related terms most commonly employed in present practice and used in this study:

| *Proposed new terminology* | *Terms used in this study* |
|---|---|
| Accrued benefit cost method | Unit credit method |
| Projected benefit cost methods: | |
|   Individual level cost methods: | |
|     Without supplemental liability | Individual level premium method |
|     With supplemental liability | Entry age normal method (individual basis) |
|   Aggregate level cost methods: | |
|     Without supplemental liability | Aggregate method |
|     With supplemental liability | Attained age normal method; entry age normal method (aggregate basis) |
| Supplemental liability | Past service cost; prior service cost |

It should be noted that the word "level," as used in the new terminology, refers to the cost recognized for each participant in successive periods, rather than to the employer's total cost for the periods. Initial conclusions of the terminology committee were presented in an article entitled "Actuarial Cost Methods—New Pension Terminology," by Joseph J. Melone, in *The Journal of Insurance*, Sept. 1963, pp. 456-464.

**Actuarial Gains (Losses).** The effects on actuarially calculated pension cost of (a) deviations between actual prior experience and the *actuarial assumptions* used or (b) changes in *actuarial assumptions* as to future events.

**Actuarial Reserve Requirement.** See *accrued actuarial liability*.

**Actuarial Soundness.** An actuarial concept relating to the degree of assurance (existing under an employer's program for funding pension cost) that the funds set aside under a pension plan will be sufficient to meet the pension payments provided for in the plan. Actuaries have not defined *actuarial soundness*.[1]

**Actuarial Valuation.** See *valuation*.

**Actuary.** A person skilled in the science of applying the probabilities of longevity to financial, insurance, or other types of calculations.

**Aggregate Level Cost Method.** See *actuarial cost method*.

**Aggregate Method.** An *actuarial cost method*. See Appendix C, p. 132.

**Annuitant.** A person entitled to receive payments under an annuity; a person receiving such payments.

**Annuity (Life Annuity).** A series of payments at fixed intervals, normally in equal amounts, continuing for the life of the recipient.

**Assumptions.** See *actuarial assumptions*.

**Attained Age Normal Method.** An *actuarial cost method*. See Appendix C, p. 133.

**Benefits (Pension Benefits) (Retirement Benefits).** The pensions and any other payments to which employees or their beneficiaries may be entitled under a pension plan.

---

[1] For a discussion of the concept, see Dorrance C. Bronson, *Concepts of Actuarial Soundness in Pension Plans*, 1957.

**Contribute.** When used in connection with a pension plan, *contribute* ordinarily is synonymous with *pay*.

**Contribution Rate.** (1) As to an employee—a factor, such as a percentage of compensation, used in determining the amounts of payments to be made by the employee under a contributory pension plan. (2) As to an employer—a factor, calculated in an actuarial valuation, to be used in determining the employer's annual *normal cost* contribution under a pension plan. An employer's *contribution rate* may be either a percentage to be applied to the total compensation paid to covered employees for a particular year or an amount in dollars to be applied to the total number of covered employees at a particular date.

**Contributory Plan.** A pension plan under which employees bear part of the cost. In some *contributory plans*, employees wishing to be covered must contribute; in other *contributory plans*, employee contributions are voluntary and result in increased benefits.

**Cost (Costs).** See *pension cost*.

**Cost-of-Living Plan.** See *variable benefit plan*.

**Covered.** A person *covered* by a pension plan is one who has fulfilled the eligibility requirements stated in the plan and (a) for whom benefits have accrued or are accruing or (b) who is receiving benefits under the plan.

**Credited Service.** Employment considered in determining an employee's eligibility to receive pension payments or in determining the amount of such payments. See *service*.

**Current Service.** See *service*.

**Current Service Cost.** Pension cost related, under the actuarial cost method in use, to current service. See *normal cost*.

**Deferred Annuity.** An annuity under which payments are to begin at some specified time in the future.

**Deferred Profit-sharing Plan.** One of several types of arrangements whereby an employer provides retirement benefits for employees. In a *deferred profit-sharing plan,* the employer makes available deferred sums based on the earnings of the business; the benefits for each employee are the amounts which can be provided by sums specifically allocated to him. A *deferred profit-sharing plan* is not a *pension plan* for purposes of this research study.

**Defined-benefit Plan.** A pension plan stating the benefits to be received by employees after retirement, or the method of determining such benefits. The employer's contributions under such a plan are determined actuarially on the basis of the benefits expected to become payable. See *defined-contribution plan*.

**Defined-contribution Plan.** (1) A pension plan which (a) states the benefits to be received by employees after retirement or the method of determining such benefits (as in the case of a defined-benefit plan) and (b) accompanies a separate agreement that provides a formula for calculating the employer's contributions (for example, a fixed amount for each ton produced or for each hour worked, or a fixed percentage of compensation). Initially, the benefits stated in the plan are those which the contributions expected to be made by the employer can provide. If later the contributions are found to be inadequate or excessive for the purpose of funding the stated benefits on the basis originally contemplated (for example, because of a change in the level of operations), either the contributions or the benefits (or both) may be adjusted in subsequent negotiations. See *defined-benefit plan*. (2) A *money-purchase plan*.

**Deposit Administration Contract.** A *funding instrument*. See Appendix C, p. 114. This type of contract is also called a *deposit administration group annuity contract*.

**Entry Age Normal Method.** An *actuarial cost method*. See Appendix C, p. 127.

**Equity Annuity Plan.** See *variable benefit plan*.

**Frozen.** Not subject to change. Ordinarily applied to *past service cost*. See *frozen initial liability*.

**Frozen Initial Liability.** Past service cost which is not changed by factors such as actuarial gains and losses and increases in plan benefits.

**Fully Funded.** A specific element of pension cost (for example, past service cost) is said to have been *fully funded* if the amount of the cost has been paid in full to a funding agency. A pension plan is said by some to be *fully funded* if regular payments are being made under the plan to a funding agency to cover the normal cost and reasonably rapid amortization of the past service cost.

**Fund.** Used as a verb, *fund* means to pay over to a funding agency (as, to *fund* future pension benefits, to *fund* pension cost). Used as a noun, *fund* refers to assets accumulated in the hands of a funding agency for the purpose of meeting retirement benefits when they become due.

**Funded.** The portion of pension cost which has been paid to a funding agency is said to have been *funded*. See *fund* (verb).

**Funding Agency.** An organization or individual, such as a specific corporate or individual trustee or an insurance company, which provides facilities for the accumulation of assets to be used for the payment of benefits under a pension plan; an organization, such as a specific life insurance company, which provides facilities for the purchase of such benefits.

**Funding Instrument.** An agreement or contract governing the conditions under which a funding agency performs its functions.

**Funding Method.** Any of several techniques which actuaries use in determining the amounts of employer contributions to provide for pension cost. An *actuarial cost method*.

**Future Service.** See *service*.

**Future Service Cost.** See *normal cost*.

**Gains.** See *actuarial gains (losses)*.

**Graded Vesting.** See *vest*.

**Group Annuity Contract.** A *funding instrument*. See Appendix C, p. 114. Also called a group deferred annuity contract.

**Immature.** Said of employee groups. See *mature*.

**Immediate Basis.** A procedure for recognizing actuarial gains and losses. See the discussion in Appendix C, p. 120.

**Immediate Participation Guarantee Contract.** A *funding instrument*. See Appendix C, p. 115.

**Individual Level Cost Method.** See *actuarial cost method*.

**Individual Level Premium Method.** An *actuarial cost method*. See Appendix C, p. 131.

**Insured Plan.** A pension plan for which the funding agency is an insurance company.

**Interest.** The return earned or to be earned on funds invested or to be invested to provide for future pension benefits. In calling the return *interest*, it is recognized that in addition to interest on debt securities the earnings of a pension fund may include dividends on equity securities, rentals on real estate and gains or (as offsets) losses on fund investments.

**Level Cost Method.** See *actuarial cost method*.

**Life Annuity.** See *annuity*.

**Life Expectancy.** Average years of remaining life after a specified age.

**Losses.** See *actuarial gains (losses)*.

**Mature.** An employee group is said to be *mature* if the age distribution of the employees, including the ages of employees who have retired and are drawing pensions, is stable and is expected to be duplicated year after year through the effect of new entries and dropouts (deaths and withdrawals). This condition is typical of a company whose pension plan has long been in effect and whose work force is neither increasing nor decreasing. Newly established companies and growing companies ordinarily have *immature* employee groups. Employee groups covered by pension plans recently adopted also tend to be *immature*.

**Money-purchase Plan.** A type of pension plan in which the employer's contributions are determined for, and allocated with respect to, specific individuals, usually as a percentage of compensation. The benefits for each employee are the amounts which can be provided by the sums contributed for him.

**Mortality Rate.** Death rate; the proportion of the number of deaths in a specified group to the number living at the beginning of the period in which the deaths occur. Actuaries use *mortality tables*, which show death rates for each age, in estimating the amount of future retirement benefits which will become payable. See *life expectancy*.

**Multi-employer Plan.** A pension plan in which two or more employers participate. This expression is not ordinarily used, however, when the employers in question are related (for example, as parent and subsidiary).

**Negotiated Plan.** A pension plan which results from collective bargaining. See *unilateral plan*.

**Noncontributory Plan.** See *contributory plan*.

**Normal Cost.** The annual cost assigned, under the actuarial cost method in use, to years subsequent to the inception of a pension plan, exclusive of any element representing a portion of the past service cost or interest thereon. See the discussions in Appendix C under specific actuarial cost (funding) methods, pp. 121 to 133. See *past service cost*.

**Participant.** An employee (active or retired) who is covered by a pension plan. See *covered*.

**Past Service.** See *service*.

**Past Service Cost.** Pension cost assigned, under the actuarial cost method in use, to years prior to the inception of a pension plan. See the discussions in Appendix C under specific actuarial cost (funding) methods, pp. 121 to 133. *Past service cost* is sometimes called *initial accrued actuarial liability*. See *normal cost, supplemental liability*.

**Pay-As-You-Go.** Paying pension benefits as they become due without advance funding. See Appendix C, p. 122.

**Pension.** A regular payment, usually monthly, to a person who has retired from employment because of advanced age or disability. Also called *retirement income*.

**Pension Benefits.** See *benefits*.

**Pension Cost(s) (Actuarial Cost).** The present value, as of the date of a valuation, of prospective benefits under a pension plan; also, the portion or portions of such present value assigned to a specific period or periods of time. The singular and plural forms are used interchangeably. See *current service cost, normal cost, past service cost, prior service cost*.

**Pension Plan (Retirement Plan).** Any of several types of arrangements whereby an employer provides benefits for employees after they retire. For the purposes of this study, the term *pension plan* comprehends both formal, written plans and plans whose existence may be implied from the existence of a well defined, although perhaps unwritten, policy on the part of the employer regarding payment of retirement benefits to employees. On the other hand, an employer's practice of making retirement payments in amounts determined arbitrarily at or after retirement to selected retired employees does not imply a *pension plan* for purposes of the study.

**Portable Pensions.** Pension entitlements that are vested and consequently accompany an employee as he moves from employer to employer are referred to as *portable pensions*. This reference is particularly applicable if the pension benefits are to be paid through a central organization.

**Present Value.** The current worth of an amount or series of amounts payable or receivable in the future. *Present value* is determined by discounting the future amount or amounts at a predetermined rate of interest. In pension plan valuations, actuaries often combine arithmetic factors representing probability (examples are factors for mortality, withdrawal, future compensation levels) with arithmetic factors representing discount (interest). Consequently, to actuaries, determining the *present value* of future pension benefits may mean applying factors of both types.

**Prior Service.** See *service*.

**Prior Service Cost.** Pension cost assigned, under the actuarial cost method in use, to years prior to the date of a particular actuarial valuation. See the discussions in Appendix C under specific actuarial cost (funding) methods, pp. 121 to 133. See *accrued actuarial liability*.

**Profit-sharing Plan.** See *deferred profit-sharing plan*.

**Projected Benefit Cost Method.** See *actuarial cost method*.

**Projection Scale.** A basis used in adjusting *mortality tables* for expected improvement in longevity.

**Retirement Benefits.** See *benefits*.

**Retirement Income.** A *pension*.

**Service.** Employment taken into consideration under a pension plan. Years of employment before the inception of a plan constitute an employee's *past service;* years thereafter are classified in relation to the particular actuarial valuation being made or discussed. Years of employment (including *past service*) prior to the date of a particular valuation constitute *prior service;* years of employment following the date of the valuation constitute *future service;* a year of employment adjacent to the date of the valuation, or in which such date falls, constitutes *current service* (included in *future service*).

**Service Life.** The entire period of an employee's service with an employer.

**Set-back.** A procedure used in adjusting a *mortality table* for improvement in longevity. In making a *set-back*, actuaries apply a mortality table as if each employee included in a calculation were one or more years younger than he actually is.

**Single-premium Method.** See *unit credit method*.

**Split Funding.** The use, under a pension plan, of more than one type of funding instrument—for example, a trust agreement or a group annuity contract.

**Spread Basis.** A procedure for recognizing actuarial gains and losses. See the discussion in Appendix C, p. 120.

**Step-rate Method.** See *unit credit method*.

**Supplemental Liability.** A separate element of actuarial cost which appears when the actuarial cost method establishes future regular cost accruals whose actuarial present value is less than the actuarial present value of the total projected benefits of . . . [a pension] plan. (Term and definition proposed by a committee of The American Risk and Insurance Association.) See *actuarial cost method*.

**Terminal Funding.** A *funding method*. See Appendix C, p. 123.

**Trust Fund Plan.** A pension plan for which the funding instrument is a trust agreement.

**Turnover.** Termination of employment for a reason other than death or retirement.

**Unfunded.** See *funded*.

**Unilateral Plan.** A pension plan which does not result from collective bargaining. See *negotiated plan*.

**Unit Credit Method.** An *actuarial cost method*. See Appendix C, p. 123.

**Valuation.** The process by which an actuary estimates the present value of benefits to be paid under a pension plan and calculates the amounts of employer contributions or accounting charges for pension cost.

**Variable Benefit Plan.** A pension plan in which the retirement benefits otherwise specified are varied from time to time to provide a measure of protection of the purchasing power of the benefits. In a *cost-of-living plan*, the benefits are adjusted to reflect variations in a specific index, such as the Consumer Price Index of the United States Bureau of Labor Statistics. In an *equity annuity plan*, the periodic benefit (or, more frequently, one-half of the benefit) is dependent on the investment experience of a specific portfolio containing equity securities.

**Vest.** An employee's right to receive a present or future pension benefit *vests* when his right eventually to receive the benefit is *no longer* contingent on his remaining in the service of the employer. (Other conditions, such as inadequacy of the pension fund, may prevent the employee from receiving the vested benefit.) Under *graded vesting*, the initial vested right may be to receive in the future a stated percentage of a pension based on the number of years of accumulated credited service; thereafter, the percentage may increase with the number of years of service or of age until the right to receive the entire benefit has vested. See *portable pensions*.

**Withdrawal.** The removal of an employee from coverage under a pension plan for a reason other than death or retirement. See *turnover*.

APPENDIX E

# Accounting Research Bulletins

*Accounting Research Bulletin No. 47,* "Accounting for Costs of Pension Plans," has been a major factor influencing the present practices of employers in accounting for pension expense. It is reproduced in this appendix. *ARB 47* was issued in 1956 by the committee on accounting procedure of the American Institute of Certified Public Accountants (then the American Institute of Accountants). Six members of the committee assented with qualification, citing Section A, "Pension Plans—Annuity Costs Based on Past Service," of Chapter 13 of *Accounting Research Bulletin No. 43,* "Restatement and Revision of Accounting Research Bulletins." That section is also reproduced in this appendix.

CHAPTER 13

## Compensation

SECTION A | *Pension Plans—Annuity Costs Based on Past Service*

1. THIS SECTION DEALS WITH the accounting treatment of costs arising out of past service which are incurred under pension plans involving payments to outside agencies such as insurance companies and trustees. Self-administered and informal plans which do not require payments to outside agencies are not dealt with because of their special features and lack of uniformity. The principles set forth herein, however, are generally applicable to those plans as well.

2. Charges with respect to pension costs based on past service have sometimes been made to surplus on the ground that such payments are indirectly compensation for services and that since the

services upon which computation of the payments is based were performed in the past, the compensation should not be permitted to affect any period or periods other than those in which the services involved were performed. In other cases all annuity costs based on past service have been charged to income in the period of the plan's inauguration as a current cost of originating the plan. In still other cases the position has been taken that a pension plan cannot bring the hoped-for benefits in the future unless past as well as future services are given recognition and, accordingly, annuity costs based on past service have been spread over a period of present and future years. The last method is the one permitted under provisions of the Internal Revenue Code.[1]

3. The committee believes that, even though the calculation is based on past service, costs of annuities based on such service are incurred in contemplation of present and future services, not necessarily of the individual affected but of the organization as a whole, and therefore should be charged to the present and future periods benefited. This belief is based on the assumption that although the benefits to a company flowing from pension plans are intangible, they are nevertheless real. The element of past service is one of the important considerations in establishing pension plans, and annuity costs measured by such past service contribute to the benefits gained by the adoption of a plan. It is usually expected that such benefits will include better employee morale, the removal of superannuated employees from the payroll, and the attraction and retention of more desirable personnel, all of which should result in improved operations.

4. The committee, accordingly, is of the opinion that:

(a) Costs of annuities based on past service should be allocated to current and future periods; however, if they are not sufficiently material in amount to distort the results of operations in a single period, they may be absorbed in the current year;

(b) Costs of annuities based on past service should not be charged to surplus.

5. This opinion is not to be interpreted as requiring that charges be made to income rather than to reserves previously provided, or that recognition be given in the accounts of current or future periods to pension costs written off prior to the issuance of an opinion on this subject.

---

[1] See IRC Sec. 23(p)(1)(A).

# Accounting Research BULLETINS

★

Issued by the
Committee on Accounting Procedure
American Institute of
Certified Public Accountants
270 Madison Avenue, New York 16, N. Y.

September, 1956     No. 47

## Accounting for Costs of Pension Plans

1. Variations in the provisions of pension plans in the United States, in their financial arrangements, and in the circumstances attendant upon their adoption, have resulted in substantial differences in accounting for pension costs. This bulletin indicates guides which, in the opinion of the committee, are acceptable for dealing with costs of pension plans in the accounts and reports of companies having such plans. It is not concerned with funding as such.

2. The term *pension plan* is here intended to mean a formal arrangement for employee retirement benefits, whether established unilaterally or through negotiation, by which commitments, specific or implied, have been made which can be used as the basis for estimating costs. It does not include profit-sharing plans or deferred-compensation contracts with individuals. It does not apply to informal arrangements by which voluntary payments are made to retired employees, usually in amounts fixed at or about the time of an employee's retirement and in the light of his then situation but subject to change or discontinuance at the employer's will; where such informal arrangements exist, the pay-as-you-go method of accounting for pension costs generally is appropriate, although the accrual method is equally appropriate in cases where costs can be estimated with reasonable accuracy.

3. When a pension plan is first adopted, it is customary to provide that pensions for covered employees will give recognition not only to services which are to be rendered by them in the future, but also to services which have been rendered by them prior to the adoption of the plan. The costs of the pensions to the employer, therefore, usually are based in part on past services and in part on current and future services of the employees. The committee considers that all of such costs are costs of doing business, incurred in contemplation of present and future benefits, as are other employment costs such as wages, salaries, and social security taxes. It, therefore, is of the opinion that past service benefit costs should be charged to operations during the current and future periods benefited, and should not be charged to earned surplus *at the inception of the plan.* The committee believes that, in the case of an *existing plan* under which inadequate charges or no charges for past services have been made thus far and the company has decided to conform its accounting to the preferred procedure expressed in this bulletin, it may be appropriate to charge to earned surplus the amount that should have been accumulated by charges to income since inception of the plan.

4. In addition to the basic features of a pension plan relating to employee eligibility and the level of pension payments, other factors enter into the determination of the ultimate costs of pensions. Some of these are:

(a) other benefits (such as social security) where amounts of pension payments are integrated therewith;

(b) length of life of employees both before and after retirement;

(c) employee turnover;

(d) in some cases, alternatives as to age at which employees may retire;

(e) future compensation levels; and

(f) in a funded plan, future rates of earnings on the fund and the status of fund investments.

Because of these factors, the total cost of the pensions that will be paid ultimately to the present participants in a plan cannot be determined precisely in advance, but, by the use of actuarial techniques, reasonably accurate estimates can be made. There are other business costs for which it is necessary to make periodic provisions in the accounts based upon assumptions and estimates. The committee believes that the uncertainties relating to the determination of pension costs are not so pronounced as to preclude similar treatment.

5. In the view of many, the accrual of costs under a pension plan should not necessarily be dependent on the funding arrangements provided for in the plan or governed by a strict legal interpretation of the obligations under the plan. They feel that because of the widespread adoption of pension plans and their importance as part of compensation structures, a provision for cancellation or the existence of a terminal date for a plan should not be the controlling factor in accounting for pension costs, and that for accounting purposes it is reasonable to assume in most cases that a plan, though modified or renewed (because of terminal dates) from time to time, will continue for an indefinite period. According to this view, costs based on current and future services should be systematically accrued during the expected period of active service of the covered employees, generally upon the basis of actuarial calculations. Such calculations may be made as to each employee, or as to categories of employees (by age, length of service, or rate of pay, for example), or they may be based upon an average of the expected service lives of all covered employees. These calculations, although made primarily for funding purposes, may be used also for accounting purposes. They should, of course, be revised at intervals. Also according to this view, costs based on past services should be charged off over some reasonable period, provided the allocation is made on a systematic and rational basis and does not cause distortion of the operating results in any one year. The length of the period benefited by costs based on past services is subject to considerable difference of opinion. Some think that the benefits accrue principally during the early years of a plan;

others feel that the period primarily benefited approximates the remaining service life of the employees covered by a plan at the time of its adoption; still others believe that the benefits of such costs extend over an indefinite period, possibly the entire life of a plan and its successors, if any. In practice, costs based on past services have in many instances been charged off over a ten- to twelve-year period, or over a fixed longer period such as twenty or thirty years. (The minimum period presently permitted for tax purposes is ten years if the initial past-service cost is immediately paid in full, or about twelve years if one-tenth of the initial past-service cost plus interest is paid each year.)

6. In the view of others, the full accrual of pension costs may be unnecessary. They point out that in some cases accounting for such costs in the manner indicated in paragraph 5 would result, as to a given year or cumulatively or both, in the accrual of costs under a pension plan in amounts differing materially from the payments made under the plan into a pension fund or to retired employees, and in other cases it would require the employer to record pension costs in amounts varying widely from his legal liabilities. They say that a company would in all probability never be called upon to utilize the entire amount of an actuarially calculated full accrual, and that, in the event of liquidation of the business, any amounts accrued with respect to employees who have not at the time acquired vested rights would, except for a voluntary act of grace, revert to the surplus of the company. They also believe that in the case of an unfunded or partially funded plan the accumulation of a substantial accrual would lead to pressure for full funding, possibly to the detriment of the company and its security holders, and that fear of this might deter management from entering into pension arrangements beneficial to employees. They also feel that the method of accounting envisioned in paragraph 5 disregards the probability that future unfavorable changes in a company's economic position undoubtedly would lead to changes in the pension arrangements it would make for its em-

ployees. According to this view, management should have wider discretion in accounting for pension costs, provided there is adequate disclosure as to the method followed.

7. The committee regards the method outlined in paragraph 5 as being the method most likely to effect a reasonable matching of costs and revenues, and therefore considers it to be preferable. However, the committee believes that opinion as to the accounting for pension costs has not yet crystallized sufficiently to make it possible at this time to assure agreement on any one method, and that differences in accounting for pension costs are likely to continue for a time. Accordingly, for the present, the committee believes that, as a minimum, the accounts and financial statements should reflect accruals which equal the present worth, actuarially calculated, of pension commitments to employees to the extent that pension rights have vested in the employees, reduced, in the case of the balance sheet, by any accumulated trusteed funds or annuity contracts purchased.

8. The committee believes that the costs of many pension plans are so material that the fact of adoption of a plan or an important amendment to it constitutes significant information in financial statements. When a plan involving material costs is adopted, there should be a footnote to the financial statements for the year in which this occurs, stating the important features of the plan, the proposed method of funding or paying, the estimated annual charge to operations, and the basis on which such annual charge is determined. When an existing plan is amended to a material extent, there should be similar disclosure of the pertinent features of the amendment. When there is a change in the accounting procedure which materially affects the results of operations, there should be appropriate indication thereof. If there are costs of material amount based on past or current services for which reasonable provision has not been, or is not being, made in the accounts, appropriate disclosure should be made in a footnote to the financial statements as long as this situation exists.

*The statement entitled "Accounting for Costs of Pension Plans" was adopted unanimously by the twenty-one members of the committee, of whom six, Messrs. Flatley, Jennings, Lindquist, Luther, Powell and Staub, assented with qualification.*

The six members assenting with qualification object to that part of paragraph 3 which appears to sanction the charging to earned surplus in some circumstances of pension costs based on past service. They believe this to be in conflict with section A of chapter 13 of Accounting Research Bulletin No. 43, in which the committee expresses the opinion that costs of annuities based on past service should not be charged to surplus. They consider the conclusions expressed in chapter 13 to be sound for the reasons therein stated.

**COMMITTEE ON ACCOUNTING PROCEDURE (1955-1956)**

| | | |
|---|---|---|
| JOHN A. LINDQUIST, Chairman | CARL H. FORSBERG | WALTER R. STAUB |
| GORDON S. BATTELLE | LeVERNE W. GARCIA | ROSS T. WARNER |
| GARRETT T. BURNS | DONALD R. JENNINGS | WILLIAM W. WERNTZ |
| ROBERT CALDWELL | WILLIAM L. KEATING | EDWARD B. WILCOX |
| ALMAND R. COLEMAN | HOMER L. LUTHER | JAMES B. WILLING |
| ROBERT L. DIXON | JOHN K. McCLARE | |
| L. T. FLATLEY | JOHN PEOPLES | CARMAN G. BLOUGH |
| THOMAS D. FLYNN | WELDON POWELL | Director of Research |

# Selected Bibliography

AARON, BENJAMIN, *Legal Status of Employee Benefit Rights under Private Pension Plans.* Richard D. Irwin, Inc. 1961.

AMERICAN ACCOUNTING ASSOCIATION. Committee on Accounting Concepts and Standards. *Accounting and Reporting Standards for Corporate Financial Statements—1957 Revision.*

AMERICAN INSTITUTE OF CERTIFIED PUBLIC ACCOUNTANTS. *Accounting Trends and Techniques,* Seventeenth Edition. 1963.

AMERICAN INSTITUTE OF CERTIFIED PUBLIC ACCOUNTANTS. Committee on Accounting Procedure. *Accounting Research and Terminology Bulletins (Final Edition).* 1961.

ARTHUR ANDERSEN & CO., *Accounting for the Costs of Pension Plans.* (Privately printed.) 1962.

ANDERSON, D. R., "An Actuary Looks at Portable Pensions," *The Canadian Chartered Accountant,* July 1963, pp. 41-44.

BAKER, ROY E., "The Pension Cost Problem," *The Accounting Review,* Jan. 1964, pp. 52-61.

BASSETT, PRESTON C., "Accounting for Pension-plan Costs on Corporate Financial Statements." *Transactions of the Society of Actuaries,* Volume XVI, 1964, pp. 318-334.

BLOUGH, CARMAN G., ed., "Accounting and Auditing Problems—Elimination of Provision for Pension Costs Unjustified," *The Journal of Accountancy,* Dec. 1958, p. 74.

BRONSON, DORRANCE C., *Concepts of Actuarial Soundness in Pension Plans.* Richard D. Irwin, Inc. 1957.

BRONSON, DORRANCE C., "Pensions—1949," *Transactions of the Society of Actuaries,* Volume I, 1949, pp. 219-294.

BRUNDAGE, PERCIVAL F., "Pension Plans from an Accountant's Point of View," *The Journal of Accountancy,* Jan. 1950, pp. 8-15.

Casey, William J., ed., *Pay Plans.* Institute for Business Planning, Inc. 1962.

Commerce Clearing House, Inc. *Pension and Profit-Sharing Plans and Clauses.* 1957.

Corbin, Donald A., "Some Basic Questions in Pension Planning," *The Controller,* Nov. 1958, pp. 530-534.

Coutts, W. B., and Dale-Harris, R. B., *Accounting for Costs of Pension Plans.* The Canadian Institute of Chartered Accountants. 1963.

Curtis, James A., "Fundamentals and Terminology of Pension Plans," *The Journal of the American Society of Chartered Life Underwriters,* Sept. 1959, pp. 258-271.

Dean, Arthur H., "Accounting for the Cost of Pensions," *Harvard Business Review,* July 1950, pp. 25-40 and Sept. 1950, pp. 102-122.

Graham, Benjamin, Dodd, David L., and Cottle, Sidney, *Security Analysis,* Fourth Edition. McGraw-Hill Book Company, Inc. 1962.

Hamilton, James A., and Bronson, Dorrance C., *Pensions.* McGraw-Hill Book Company, Inc. 1958.

Harbrecht, Paul P., *Pension Funds and Economic Power.* The Twentieth Century Fund. 1959.

Haskins & Sells, *The Pension System in the United States.* (Privately printed.) 1964.

*Inland Steel Co. v. National Labor Relations Board,* 170 F. 2d 247 (C.A. 7 1948) cert. den., 336 U.S. 960, (1949).

Institute of Life Insurance. *Private and Public Pension Plans in the United States.* 1963.

Jenkins, David O., "Accounting for Funded Industrial Pension Plans," *The Accounting Review,* July 1964, pp. 648-653.

Lorensen, Leonard, "Pension Costs in Selected Financial Statements," *The Journal of Accountancy,* March 1962, pp. 57-61.

Lybrand, Ross Bros. & Montgomery, *Fundamental Concepts Underlying Pension Plan Financing and Costs.* (Privately printed.) 1964.

Matthews, Roy M., Jr., "Accounting for Pension Costs," *NAA Bulletin,* Aug. 1960, pp. 19-26.

McGill, Dan M., *Fundamentals of Private Pensions,* Second Edition. Richard D. Irwin, Inc. 1964.

McGill, Dan M., *Fulfilling Pension Expectations.* Richard D. Irwin, Inc. 1962.

McNulty, James E., Jr., *Decision and Influence Processes in Private Pension Plans.* Richard D. Irwin, Inc. 1961.

Melone, Joseph J., "Actuarial Cost Methods—New Pension Terminology," *The Journal of Insurance,* Sept. 1963, pp. 456-464.

Moonitz, Maurice, *Accounting Research Study No. 1,* "The Basic Postulates of Accounting." American Institute of Certified Public Accountants. 1961.

PATTERSON, EDWIN W., *Legal Protection of Private Pension Expectations.* Richard D. Irwin, Inc. 1960.

PRESIDENT'S COMMITTEE ON CORPORATE PENSION FUNDS AND OTHER PRIVATE RETIREMENT AND WELFARE PROGRAMS. *Public Policy and Private Pension Programs—A Report to the President on Private Employee Retirement Plans.* U. S. Government Printing Office. Jan. 1965.

SCOTT, S. R., "Accounting Features of Pension Plans," *The Canadian Chartered Accountant,* Aug. 1963, pp. 90-95.

SLOAT, FREDERICK P., "Valuation of Equities Held in Retirement Plan Trust Funds," *Lybrand Journal,* Volume 45, Number 4, 1964, pp. 38-50.

SPROUSE, ROBERT T., and MOONITZ, MAURICE, *Accounting Research Study No. 3,* "A Tentative Set of Broad Accounting Principles for Business Enterprises." American Institute of Certified Public Accountants. 1962.

TROWBRIDGE, CHARLES L., "The Unfunded Present Value Family of Pension Funding Methods," *Transactions of the Society of Actuaries,* Volume XV, 1963, pp. 151-192.

TROWBRIDGE, CHARLES L., "Fundamentals of Pension Funding," *Transactions of the Society of Actuaries,* Volume IV, 1952, pp. 17-43.

UNITED STATES DEPARTMENT OF LABOR, BUREAU OF LABOR STATISTICS, *Labor Mobility and Private Pension Plans.* U.S. Government Printing Office. 1964.

UNITED STATES SECURITIES AND EXCHANGE COMMISSION, Annual Report. 1952, p. 34; 1951, p. 164; 1950, pp. 16, 157; 1949, p. 20; and 1947, pp. 23, 123.

UNITED STATES SECURITIES AND EXCHANGE COMMISSION, *Statistical Bulletin,* June 1962.

WILLIAMS, JOHN H., "Actuarial Principles and Pension Plans," *The New York Certified Public Accountant,* July 1959, pp. 505-515 and Aug. 1959, pp. 578-584.

ARTHUR YOUNG & COMPANY, *Tax Aspects of Deferred Compensation.* (Privately printed.) 1963.